The Celtic Year

Shirley Toulson, who lives in Somerset, was drawn into the spell of Celtic Christianity as she worked on her books dealing with the oldest roads and folklore of Britain and Ireland, and found herself following the routes taken on their journeys by the saints of the early church.

The Celtic Year

A MONTH-BY-MONTH CELEBRATION OF
CELTIC CHRISTIAN FESTIVALS AND SITES

SHIRLEY TOULSON

ELEMENT

Shaftesbury, Dorset ● Rockport, Massachusetts
Brisbane, Queensland

Published in Great Britain in 1993 by
Element Books Limited
Longmead, Shaftesbury, Dorset

Published in the USA in 1993 by
Element, Inc
42 Broadway, Rockport, MA 01966

Published in Australia in 1993 by
Element Books Limited for
Jacaranda Wiley Limited
33 Park Road, Milton, Brisbane 4064

Reprinted December 1993

Illustrated by Brian Partridge
Maps by Taurus Graphics
Cover design by Max Fairbrother
Text designed by Roger Lightfoot
Typeset by The Electronic Book Factory Ltd, Fife, Scotland
Printed and bound in Great Britain by
Redwood Books Ltd, Trowbridge, Wiltshire

British Library Cataloguing in Publication
data available

Library of Congress Cataloguing in Publication
data available

ISBN 1–85230–361–1

 # CONTENTS

For Jane Whittle,
green friend and adopted Celt

 # How to Use this Book

Unless this book should fall into your hands at the beginning of November, it is not one that should be read from start to finish; although I do suggest that you read the introduction before taking it up at the appropriate season.

You will not find that it necessarily supplies daily readings, for several saints' festivals may fall on the same date, while other days will be blank. My aim in linking the Celtic saints to the Celtic year has been a different one: I have hoped to help the reader become more aware of times and seasons. For this reason I have thought in months rather than in days, and I hope that the appropriate saints' entries together with the poems, blessings and the decorative illustrations will form a twelve-linked spiral, enabling the reader to draw further insights each successive year.

As well as linking the lives of the saints to the seasons in which they are celebrated, I have, wherever possible, stressed the importance of the places (whose locations I have given as precisely as possible) where the early Celtic saints are most keenly remembered. All places are holy, if we will only keep ourselves aware of where we are, but the hermitages, caves, holy wells and ruined oratories associated with the Celtic saints are both numinous in themselves and instrumental in awakening us to the general sanctity of earth and water. For this reason you will find a suggested pilgrimage to a holy site each month.

The journeys that you will undertake are not however purely a matter of geography. I want to stress that on a much more significant level this should be a book that its readers create as they make it part of their own inner journeys. So, I trust that it may serve as a useful guide on both your temporal and your spiritual pilgrimages; and that it will enable you, in the companionship of the Celtic saints you will meet in its pages, to embark on your own explorations.

In doing so, you will be led into the realms of symbol and metaphor, much beloved of the early medieval monks who wrote many of the first lives of the Celtic saints, basing them on traditions handed down through generations. To take literally the words and the stories that I quote is to enter a Wonderland of quaint absurdities. I ask you instead to break through the Looking Glass and come towards the meaning behind the symbols. Where it is appropriate, I have spelt that meaning out, but often the true significance is destroyed if a metaphor is pinned down too firmly, as a poem is lost in a prose paraphrase. So there are many cases where an inner truth will only reveal itself to patient contemplation.

Finally, there are two practical considerations to remember before you embark on this book. Firstly you will find that there are often several ways in which a saint's name can be spelt. I have usually given the most well-known version in such cases, but you may come across others. You may also find differing opinions as to the dates of the festivals. This is partly because the saints' days suffered in the general confusion caused by Britain adopting the Gregorian calendar in September 1752, when the third of that month became the fourteenth, and eleven days were lost; and partly because in the Middle Ages the important trading fairs of each town were granted by charter linked to the festival of the saint to whom the parish church was dedicated. In the latter case it is understandable, especially if the saint was only honoured locally, that a few calendar adjustments might be made in the interests of convenience. In most cases the saints' festivals are celebrated on the days of their deaths; but in a few cases, noted in the text if it is known, the saint's day will fall on the day that the relics were enshrined.

 # Acknowledgements

I am grateful to the following individuals and publishers for permission to quote from their works.

John Montague, 'The Muse of Amergin', from *The Faber Book of Irish Verse*, by permission of John Montague.

Austin Clarke, 'The Blackbird of Derrycairn', by permission of R. Dardis Clarke, Dublin.

James Simmons, 'A Hermit's Song', from *The Faber Book of Irish Verse*, by permission of James Simmons.

'Collect for St Hilda's Day', from *Women Included: The St Hilda Community*, by permission of SPCK.

 # Introduction

That which is called the Christian Religion existed among the Ancients, and never did not exist, from the beginning of the Human Race until Christ came in the flesh, at which time true religion, which already existed began to be called Christianity.

St Augustine

Without going back to the 'beginning of the Human Race', I would like to introduce this celebration of the Celtic Christian year by looking at its distant origins in the Bronze Age, among the peoples who inhabited these islands before the coming of the iron-forging Celts. They were the people who left the great stone monuments and ritual henges all along the Atlantic seaboard; and who buried their honoured dead in complex, majestic barrows, now mostly grassed over.

These barrows, and the artefacts found in the excavated graves within them, are almost all we know of these early farmers whose ritual monuments make it clear that they had a highly organized society and were capable of astounding feats of technology. It is our loss that they seem to have had no written language; and that although their stone and wooden circles, so carefully aligned on aspects of sunrise and sunset, were obviously of great religious significance, we can only guess at the ritual they enshrined.

In Scotland, traces of the Bronze Age culture emerge more strongly in another mysterious people, the Picts. They are believed to be the descendants of the Bronze Age people who lived in what we now call Scotland, and who intermarried with the Celts when the first waves of iron-using Celts came north. Like the people of the Bronze Age, the Picts, who appear to have been more racially akin to the Welsh than to the Scots or Irish, left no written record of their history. But we do know that they adhered to a matrilinear system of inheritance, in which a nephew (always the sister's son) was the heir. This system is not found in other Celtic societies, and is believed to have been a Bronze Age custom.

Certainly it is in the land of the Picts (that is, the eastern part of Scotland) that further evidence comes to us about the Bronze Age peoples. Like the Celts, who superseded them, they were a warlike people, who found it necessary to build hilltop forts from which they could protect their territory and which they could use as stockades where their cattle would be safe from rustlers and wild beasts. Here, in eastern Scotland, their technology led to the construction of vitrified forts, such as the royal palace of Craig Phadrig near Inverness. In these ramparts you can still find clinkers of vitrified stone, evidence that the original walls were impacted with timber, which was then set alight as a way of welding the fortifications into a mass of impenetrable strength.

The technology displayed in such buildings makes it hard to imagine that the remnants of Bronze Age people throughout Britain could easily be reduced to trembling fugitives, sheltering round the barrows and burial mounds of their ancestors, totally beaten into submission with the iron implements forged by the Celtic smiths. Many of them, as we have seen in the case of the Picts, intermarried with the new settlers. Those who remained apart were to become the stuff of folklore.

For the Irish they were the *sidh*, tomb dwellers, beings connected with the Other World, whose malign influence could be neutralized by the touch of cold iron. Much later they were to become the little people: leprechauns, pixies and fairies, mischievous creatures whose help could be bought with offerings of food and drink.

More significantly, in Irish lore they were said to be the Milesians or Sons of Mil, a people believed to have come to Ireland after the god-like Tuatha de Danaan, arriving from some mysterious land 'beyond the ninth wave'. In the Celtic *Lebor Gabala*, a book of origins, they are said to have come from Egypt, and to have seen Ireland from a tall tower which they built in Spain. This is an important speculation to remember when we come to consider the Coptic influence on Celtic Christianity.

The Milesians are said to have taken over the gods of the Tuatha whom they replaced: Dagda, the father of all the gods, possessed of perfect knowledge; and Cailleach, the Old Wise Woman, whose inclusive knowledge was of a different nature leading into the realms of prophecy. In Scottish lore the Cailleach meets Dagda in Glen Etive on the Eve of Samhain, and from their union, the power of the gods was born. When the Sons of Mil took over the land of the Tuatha, the latter were given that part of Ireland which lay underground, so the gods themselves were in a sense dwellers in the *sidh*, occupants of the world of eternity, visible only to a few seers, although all sensitive beings could be conscious of them. We will see how these ancient gods of Ireland, and their counterparts in mainland Britain, were to influence the incoming Celts and become embodied in Celtic Christianity, as figures of power, fertility and wisdom.

The migrating Celtic tribes took over the lands of the Bronze Age peoples of Britain during the first millenium BC. The long-boned, fair-haired warriors actually came to Ireland about 400 BC, settling themselves in what we now know as County Antrim, and calling it Dal-righ-phada, the place of the tall king. It was a name that they were later to give to their kingdom on the west coast of Scotland.

Like the Bronze Age people before them, the Celts were a tribal race, continually needing to defend territory from rival tribes and marauding groups. So, on the ground, the most direct evidence that we have of Celtic civilization, until about 400 CE (Common Era: a reckoning that I prefer to AD as being less divisive from other faiths – it will therefore be used throughout this book) is to be found in the extensive ramparts of their hill forts and defended encampments. There are numerous examples of these throughout Britain, but for the purposes of this study I would like to look at two which have special bearing on the evolution of Celtic Christianity. They are Tara in Ireland and Dunadd in Argyll.

Tara, standing on ground rising to a mere 300 feet (90 m) to the north-west of Dublin, appears to crown an impressive eminence, surrounded as it is by the plains of Meath. An ancient fortified site, this hill was to become the sacred palace of the Kings of Ireland. Here, where a barrow decorated with stones carved with swirling patterns indicates that this was a place to which the people of the Bronze Age brought their illustrious dead for burial, are earthen banks outlining the Great Hall where Patrick is meant to have confronted the Druids, and from which Columcille's great ancestor, Niall of the Nine Hostages, issued his edicts.

Columcille, himself, was to play a part in accentuating the significance of Dunadd, the Royal Seat of the Irish Kings who made their kingdom of Dalraida (Dal-righ-phada) in Argyll. South of Kilmartin, by the Crinan Canal, in an area rich in Bronze Age cairns and stone circles, the rocky outcrop of Dunadd (the fort by the River Add) emerges from the surrounding moss.

Its fortifications incorporate the natural rock and you reach the summit through a natural cleft. Its walls are built round terraces that are a part of the geological strata.

Just below the summit of Dunadd, on the northern part of the outcrop, you will find stones marked with the carved strokes of the Ogham script, so far undeciphered. In this case that is particularly tantalizing, for as Marion Campbell, the Kintyre archaeologist, points out, these inscriptions do not seem to be cast in the same mode as the others which are known to us, and which are invariably simply memorials naming a tribal leader.

On the summit of Dunadd, you will also find a basin cut into the rock, and beside it the carving of a wild boar, its style resembling features of the carvings on Pictish stones. This makes it clear that before the Irish came to Scotland, the Picts extended their territory west, and ruled it from this hill. Most moving of all the relics on Dunadd are two hollowed footprints, one bare, one shod, and both pointing towards the distant mountain of Ben Cruachan.

Tradition has it that the bare footprint in the Dunadd rock was made by Fergus in 500 CE when he was crowned as the first King of Dalraida, and that thereafter part of the ceremony of coronation had the new monarch placing his foot where his ancestor had stood. Furthermore, Fergus brought a stone to the site with him, and this was no less than the pillow on which Jacob had rested when he dreamt of the ladder ascending to Heaven. The stone was set by a magic cauldron (the rock basin) which always produced exactly the right amount of food for the people needing sustenance at any given time. It was here, by Fergus' stone of destiny that Columcille officiated at the crowning of a King of Dalraida, shortly after he came to Iona.

Apart from these royal palaces and the numerous tribal hill forts, the Celtic people settled in lake villages, such as those beneath Glastonbury Tor in Somerset, and on artificial islands or 'crannogs'. Around Inverness there are many traces of such island dwellings, for although the huts rot away, the islands themselves, although often totally submerged beneath the waters, are almost indestructible. Probably the best known crannog is in the lake of Llangorse in the Brecon Beacons National Park in Wales. When a Christian settlement was founded on the southern shores of that lake, the crannog was still inhabited. By the Middle Ages, it had given rise to tales of a submerged city, whose roofs and walls glinted when the rays of the sun penetrated the surface of the water.

That story reminds us that we must beware of romanticizing the pagan Celts. They were slave owners, buying and selling their prisoners of war and the remnants of the indigenous Bronze Age peoples; they plundered the lands and cattle of opposing tribes and raped their women; they decorated their great halls with the severed heads of their enemies; and they kept persistent blood feuds going for generations. Yet they had a rigid system of contractual law, reducing almost all elements of life, including their relationship to the gods, to a legal bargain. Most penalties for the breaking of a contract were reckoned in heads of cattle, but there was a loophole. So strong was the Celtic belief in the immortality of the soul that the payments of some debts could be postponed to the after-life.

The laws might be laid down by the kings and tribal leaders, but they were formulated on the advice of the Druids, who also acted as judges, for they were statesmen and councillors as well as priests. Their name is said to come from the Greek *drys*, an oak tree, although it is also claimed that it derives from the Sanskrit *veda* – to know or see. Whichever derivation is correct, the Druids certainly made their temples in oak groves, where the trees supported the sacred mistletoe, and where the oak apples could be ground into a flour that appears to have been used in a ritual meal.

We know that the Druids were people of immense learning, who had spent some twenty years in training. It is significant that the same amount of time was usually spent by the Christian saints in preparation for the main work of their lives. Much of the training of a Druid went into the memorizing of the rituals of their religion, for nothing of their sacred lore was allowed to be committed to writing – although for other purposes they wrote in both Latin and Greek.

In folklore, Druids have the powers of a shaman, being able to change their shapes at will, travel through time, and control the weather, notably by calling down mists and so rendering themselves invisible. In many stories of the lives of the saints, such as the account of Columcille's encounter with the Pictish King Brude at the palace of Craig Phadrig, the holy men engage the Druids of a powerful pagan ruler in contests of magic. Such stories indicate that for the mass of the people the wandering Christian leaders had druidic status.

The Picts were the last of the Celtic tribes in Britain to become Christians. Before the Irish came to Scotland, they are said to have inhabited lands that stretched from Shetland to the Forth of Clyde

and from the east coast to the outer isles of the west. Gradually
the Picts merged with the Irish Scots and, although by the tenth
century the King of all Scotland was a Pict, they were to lose
their national identity almost completely. Like the Druids, they
left no writing in their own language, but scholars believe that
they spoke a tongue somewhat similar to Welsh. One of the few
words that can be assigned to them is 'Urquhart', which means
woodland, and which survives in the naming of the wooded area
of Glen Urquhart by Loch Ness.

Like the Celts of Cornwall and Brittany, part of their ritual
seems to have involved carefully aligned underground passages,
'fougous' or 'sous-terrains'. In the twelfth century CE, an Icelandic
writer tried to explain these elaborate well-paved blind tunnels by
describing their use. He tells us that the Picts were small men,
who did wonders in the mornings, but who lost their strength at
mid-day, when the sun had passed its zenith, and that they then
went underground.

What we know of the Picts directly comes from the intricately
carved stones that they left behind them, and which were possibly
part of a religious ritual. Although they had a druidic culture, the
Picts' occasional use of cup and ring markings suggest that much of
their ritual came from their Bronze Age ancestors. This is certainly
not to suggest that they were in any way lacking in sophistication;
for we know that they were cunning silversmiths. Evidence for
that comes comes from the hoards of Pictish silverware discovered
in Shetland; and there seems to be no doubt that Pictish influence
instigated the long tradition of silversmithing around Inverness.

Yet it is the carved stones, some of which are dated as late as the
ninth century, which are the chief memorial to the Pictish art and
imagination. Collections of these stones can be seen at St Vigeans
and Meigle, north of Coupar Angus and three of them stand by the
roadside by the village of Aberlemno between Forfar and Brechin
in Angus. Three different motifs are combined in these carvings:
Christian symbolism; vivid and realistic scenes of contemporary
life portraying hunts and battles; and a mysterious iconography
composed of a Z-shaped rod, a character that has been described as
a mirror and a comb, and a long-snouted swimming beast, which
looks like an elephant save that its trunk protrudes from between
its ears.

These Pictish symbol stones, as they are called, have nearly
all been found by the sites of early Christian churches; and it is
generally agreed that there are many parallels between the Pictish

symbols and the intricate designs of manuscripts, such as the *Book of Kells*, prepared in the early Celtic monasteries.

It is possible that the Pictish symbols told stories and made prophecies, a function that belonged to the Celtic bards, men and women, who like the Druids were held in the highest honour in the tribes, although their functions were quite different. The *fili* or bard was primarily a praise-singer, and one who captured the folk memory of his or her tribe in stories and prophetic utterances. In order to fulfil this role, the bards, like the Druids, had to undergo a long and arduous training.

This was an aspect of the vocation of the *fili* that goes back to the Bronze Age, for we know of at least one poet among the Sons of Mil. He was Amairgen, who originated a poem affirming the unity of all creation and praising the land of Eire. This particular aspect of the God-given power of poetry was to flourish throughout the Celtic church, materializing in the seventh century in the great hymn to the creation, composed by the Anglo-Saxon Caedmon, the unlikely, tongue-tied cowherd, who lived as a lay brother in the abbey of Whitby, which was ruled by Hilda according to the Irish tradition of Iona. Probably the best-known bard today is the sixth-century Welsh Taliesin, a contemporary of King Arthur and supposedly living at the time of the flowering of the Celtic church.

His story embodies both the druidic belief in reincarnation and the shamanistic power of shape-shifting. According to his legend, the witch Ceridwen prepared a potion in her cauldron which had to simmer for a year, at the end of which time it would have boiled down to three drops which would convey the power of discerning the past, the present and the future on anyone who tasted them. To the witch's dismay, these powerful drops bubbled out of her cauldron and landed on the finger of the lad whose job it was to tend the fire. Instinctively he put his finger into his mouth to ease his pain.

Realizing what he done and and perceiving Ceridwen's fury, the boy ran away, changing himself first into a hare, then into a fish, then into a bird and finally into a grain of wheat in an endeavour to put her off the track. In turn, she chased him in the forms of a greyhound, an otter and a hawk. Foiled in those guises, she became a hen and in that form she swallowed the grain of wheat. Thus she became pregnant with the spirit of the lad who had swallowed the three prophetic drops, and in time gave birth to him in the form of the poet, Taliesin.

His poems, collected in the medieval *Book of Taliesin*, affirm him as a timeless being, who has existed from the beginning and will live until Doomsday, a 'teacher to all Christendom'. Contemporary with the writings of the Celtic saints, the poems of Taliesin are among the earliest recorded Celtic verses. Of course it is quite likely that no such individual existed and, just as Arthur may be an amalgam of several well-loved, powerful Celtic kings, so Taliesin may well be the personification of some mythical, ideal bard to whom all the early scraps of Welsh poetry were attributed. For our purpose, the important thing is that he embodied the spirit of poetry, which gives a power and significance to words beyond their literal meaning. We will find much the same power in the Celtic blessings on the activities of each day, and in the words of protection, both of which were in common use until the early years of the twentieth century.

The blessings relate to the activities that take place each day from tending the fire in the morning to 'smooring' it at night, that is covering it with peat so that it will smoulder gently until the greater heat is needed again. There are blessings on dressing, washing, preparing food, tending cattle and growing corn, most of them activities that relate particularly to women. Moreover it is the women, throughout the centuries, who played a major part in keeping these blessings alive; and it was they who provided the main source for Alexander Carmichael's researches, when that indefatigable nineteenth-century Scot set about collecting the folk songs and incantations of the Highlands and Islands.

In myth too, there are figures of women poets who can hold their own with Amairgen and Taliesin. Greatest among them is the semi-immortal figure of the Hag of Beare, whose name comes from the peninsula in West Munster where she is said to have originated. As the Cailleach, she was also known in Scotland, where she was acclaimed as late as the 1940s in the *West Highland Tales* collected by J. G. McKay. Like Taliesin, she was a shape-shifter, passing seven times through a period of youth and outliving seven husbands. A prophetess of doom, she foretold global disasters such as depleted forests and seas empty of fish that strike all too closely to our own time.

As well as taking on the role of prophet, the poets were also story-tellers, entertaining the tribal leaders through the long winter evenings, so preserving the myths and legends of the tribe. Every night from Samhain to Beltaine, that is during the dark months of the year, the poet Forgoll is said to have told a story to Mongán,

King of Ulster. The fact that these stories were told around the fire gave them an added significance, for to all tribal peoples the central hearth is sacred.

In the traditional stories that have come down to us about the lives of the saints, we find that in folklore at any rate they were credited with many of the qualities of the Druids and the bards. We know too from the illuminated manuscripts that have come down to us that they were either themselves artists of outstanding graphic ability and skill or that they must have been knowledgeable enough to support imaginative craftsmen in their monasteries. I have already explained that we often find traces of Bronze Age culture in the swirling spiral patterns of the eternal knots of Celtic art.

Such motifs in the so-called carpet pages of Celtic manuscripts also have an obvious affinity with the non-representational art of the Near East. At the same time the Celtic representation of the human form echoes the symbolic majesty of Byzantine icons. Only when the artists put plants and animals, such as you will see in the *Book of Kells*, into the margins of their pages, did the Celtic illuminators allow naturalism to break in.

As well as being glorified in its manuscript art, the Celtic church was also enriched by the works of craftsmen in metal, as the bell shrines and croziers in Dublin's National Museum will show you. These sixth-century craftsmen were following a long tradition that once again goes back to the Bronze Age. For the earliest Celtic art proves that it was from those people that the Celts learnt the skill of enamelling bronze in vivid colours.

Colours fade through the centuries, but contemporary accounts confirm that in their clothes and household furnishings, the Celts favoured brilliance of colour and design. It is against the most sumptuous trappings that we must contrast the simplicity of the beehive huts and cave hermitages in which the monks of the Celtic church spent much of their lives. We must remember too that these ascetic men and women often came from rich and noble families.

The Celtic saints turned away from the riches of the tribal leaders, but the folklore of the druidic people remained with their Christian heirs. I should like to consider three aspects of pagan Celtic lore which were to play an important role in the lives of the saints as they have come down to us. These aspects are: the significance of the severed head; the holiness of water; and the instinctual powers of animals.

For the Celts, the whole power of a person resided in the head. If you cut off your enemy's head you not only deprived him of his ability to harm you; you also acquired for yourself all the wisdom, energy and strength which he had manifested in his life. This is why the great halls of the hill forts were adorned with severed heads. It also explains why so many of the lives of the saints conclude with a beheading.

In these hagiographies, the beheaded saint often has the power to carry his head some way from the spot of his martyrdom. We are reminded of the Green Knight who rode into Arthur's court with his head beneath his arm. Always the beheading is associated with water, either by the rising of a spring at the place where the head falls to the ground, or with an already existing well, which acquires healing properties as the bleeding head is washed in it.

At the most mundane, practical level, it is easy to understand why wells came to be regarded as sacred by pagans and Christians alike. Declaring them sacrosanct was a sure way of seeing to it that the water should remain unpolluted by cattle or straying animals. So it is ironic that, because animals have such a sure instinct for knowing where water is to be found, we often hear of the actual site of a Christian settlement being determined by oxen or pigs.

The pig has a particular significance in Celtic mythology. The wild boar could be a totem animal and the symbol of the Cailleach in her role as the hag of winter. So to kill a boar was to end the winter and bring back the spring. In Wales, the great boar to be hunted is the Twrch Trwyth, who has a part to play in Arthurian legend. One tale tells us that the hunt for this creature began in Ireland and continued throughout the south-west of Britain until it reached Cornwall.

In Scotland, where the whirlpool of Corryvrechan in the waters off the coast of Jura represented the entrance to the underworld, a sow is said to have escaped through the swirling waters. She swam to land through the turbulence, and there gave birth to nine piglets (the Twrch Trwyth fathered seven), one of whom grew into the boar, whose poisoned bristle penetrated the vulnerable heel of the otherwise invulnerable boar-killer, the hero Diarmid.

So in Celtic lore, there is obviously an ambiguous attitude towards swine. They would seem to represent both the uncontrolled and destructive forces of nature and its supportive elements. In the mythology of the Celtic church it is the latter that predominates; and missionary saints like Brannoc of Braunton in north

Devon founded their settlements in a location indicated by a litter of pigs.

From their druidic forebears the Celtic Christians also inherited a love of the land, and a feeling of the unity of all creation. In this aspect, the philosophy embedded in the Celtic church bore a strong resemblance to that of the Orthodox church today, which emphasizes the sanctity of matter.

In one important way, this close relation to the created universe influenced the Celtic division of time, which appears to differ from that adopted by the Bronze Age farmers. From the alignments of stone circles, standing stones and long barrows, we know that Bronze Age builders paid particular attention to the seasons of solstice and equinox. These, however, do not coincide with the natural turning points of the seasons, which fall at points mid-way between each solstice and equinox. The Celtic year begins in November at the fallow time of the agricultural cycle, the start of winter, a time of death, darkness and rest. It wakes up in February when the light strengthens and the days begin to lengthen; bursts into growth and summer on 1 May; and concludes with the gathering of the harvest. Like the Jews, the Celts counted their days as beginning at sunset, so that the times of darkness always come before the times of light and Celts and Jews both start their New Year at the beginning of winter between the autumn equinox and the solstice.

This resemblance in the reckoning of time, reminds us how much Celtic Christianity was open to the influence of first-century Judaism; and if we look closely we will see that the prayers and blessings of the Celtic church, rescued for posterity in the nineteenth century by Alexander Carmichael and so widely quoted and used today, resemble the supplications in the Jewish prayer book. In both instances, prayers are always related to specific events and seasons. For example, the Jewish prayer for the beginning of each month, which begins 'Our God and God of our Fathers, renew this month unto us' and concludes 'Blessed art Thou, O Lord, who sanctifiest the beginnings of the months', would be completely appropriate to the spirit of Celtic prayer and to the Celtic notion of time.

Jewish prayers for the start of a journey, for the daily activities of house and field also closely parallel the Celtic prayers and blessings you will find in this book. For like the Celts, the Jews are convinced of the sanctity of all aspects of life. In our own day Martin Buber expounded on the teaching of the Hasidic doctrine that everything contains a hidden significance that becomes apparent to those who are truly awake. So: 'The people we live with or meet with, the animals that help us with our farmwork, the soil we till, the materials we shape, the tools we use, they all contain a mysterious spiritual substance, which depends on us for helping it towards its pure form, its perfection. If we neglect this spiritual substance sent across our path, if we think only of momentary purposes, without developing a genuine relationship to the beings and things in whose life we ought to take part, as they in ours, then we shall ourselves be debarred from true fulfilled existence.' We will find a similar philosophy imbued in the teachings of the saints.

There is one other aspect of Judaism which is mirrored in Celtic Christianity: the power of the feminine presence of God. Although in Jewish orthodoxy, women are regulated to an inferior position in the synagogue, that has long been changed in the Reform Movement; and Hochmah, the spirit of wisdom, and the nurturing Shekinnah have always been venerated as aspects of the divine. Like Julian of Norwich's mothering God, the feminine qualities of God are realized as a nurturing presence equal to the masculine aspect of God the creator. In the Celtic church, we will find such reverence given to the mysterious, many-faceted figure of Brigid, the Mary of the Gael.

Both Jews and Celts believe firmly in angels as messengers of God. The Celtic belief is that each one of us has a guardian angel who watches over us from the time of our birth and escorts us through the threshold of death. If we are attentive during our life-time, we will receive intimations of the divine through the intimations brought to us by our angels. In both the Old and the New Testaments, we find stories of angelic intervention in the lives of people; and from the Dead Sea Scrolls (which tell us something of the philosophy of the Essenes) we know that the community was constantly aware of the angelic hierarchy and built its liturgy around a communion with the angels. In the lives of the Celtic saints we will find many stories of encounters with angels. They may appear as heavenly visions, or they can take on a mundane human form, like the angel in the guise of a travel-worn way-farer, who appeared to Cuthbert when he was guest master at Ripon.

All these links between Judaism and the Celtic church remind us that Celtic Christianity, unlike that brought into Britain by the legions, had a direct connection with the *minims* of the early church, the first Christians who still attended the synagogue and who thought of themselves primarily as Jews.

This influence reached Ireland from Alexandria, travelling along the Atlantic seaboard from North Africa and the coasts of Spain and France, brought by traders and wandering scholars. In this way the Celts were offered a form of Christianity which differed in many respects from that which infiltrated Britain from the converts among the occupying legions. That is why we find that the Christian settlements in Ireland, Scotland, Wales and later in Cornwall and Brittany, had more in common with the Coptic church of Egypt than with the para–military, quasi–imperial hierarchy developed in Rome.

In the latter part of the first century CE and in the following decades Alexandria was the centre of learning and religious debate. It was here that the leading Jewish Rabbis settled after the destruction of the Temple and the Roman overthrow of Jerusalem. It was here too, that the Christian Fathers formulated the doctrines of the church, while remaining for many years in dialogue with the Jewish leaders. Greek was the *lingua franca* of the learned debates that took place in the Egyptian city; but before the authority of Constantinople and Rome were established, a Christian authority which was to form the church of Ethiopia and Egypt used the language of the Pharaohs, called Coptic by the Arabs, to formulate their liturgies. As the Romans were to claim Peter as the founder of the Catholic church, the Copts looked to Mark, who is traditionally said to have made the first Egyptian convert when he healed the hand of a cobbler. Clement of Alexandria claimed that Mark wrote his original gospel in that city, after the death of Peter. In that lost text, Clement found passages of spiritual teaching, which for the initiated reader could lead to 'the innermost sanctuary of truth'. These different levels in understanding biblical texts start from a concentration on the literal and ethical meaning, go on to allegorical revelations, and culminate in direct confrontations with the divine purpose. Such division could clearly lead to a Gnostic hierarchy bringing the corporate body of the church into conflict with an uncontrollable elite guided by individual insights.

By the fourth century, the church in Egypt was torn apart by the Arians (followers of Arius of Libya) who stressed the humanity of Jesus in contrast to the power of the cosmic Christ. That doctrine was contended by those, having much in common with the early Gnostics, who stressed the divinity of Jesus at the expense of His humanity. Although that later heresy of Monophysitism was quashed by the Council of Chalcedon in 451, it was to have a profound effect on the outlook of the Coptic, and thence of the Celtic, church. Indeed rather than adhere to the ruling of the Council, some of the most dedicated adherents of Monophysitism fled from Egypt, and some of them most surely travelled west and north to Ireland.

They were certainly not the first Christians to venture out of Egypt into Celtic lands, bringing with them their own experiences of Egyptian monasticism and the tradition of desert hermitages. This was a form of religious life that was to be followed by many of the Celtic saints who appear in this book. The austerities practised by the hermits of the Egyptian desert, which were to have such an influence on the Irish church, began after 313, when Constantine adopted Christianity as the official religion of Rome. This easy acceptance by officialdom did not suit the ardent nature of the Coptic monks and nuns, who wanted to test their devotion to God by living lives of the utmost frugality and simplicity, apart from the world for which they prayed.

These early desert hermits often lived in small communities made up of separate huts gathered round a common water supply. The first such clusters of cells were settled at Scete in the Nile Delta and it was a pattern to be followed by many early Celtic Christian communities. The Celtic hermits, like the desert hermits, cultivated the land around their huts in order to grow the food they needed, and apart from that time-consuming work spent their days in prayer.

Like the Jews, the hermits of the Coptic church stood to pray, elbows close to their sides and palms uplifted. In this way the saints of the Celtic church also made their daily recitals of the psalter, using the biblical words as a way of centring and stilling the mind, and keeping the continual procession of passing thoughts at bay.

Yet we would be wrong to imagine that there was a division between formal prayer and manual work. Indeed the hermits of the Egyptian desert were known to set themselves feats of apparently useless drudgery if no appropriate work was to hand. In this way they would use repetitive tasks to still their minds and empty them of worldly concerns. More relevant to the attitudes adopted by the Celtic church, as we have seen, was that of dedicating every activity to God's purpose, and being constantly aware and responsible in every aspect of daily life and work. In the Celtic blessings and prayers, we find a constant echo of the Essene advocacy of constant worship formulated by the Egyptian

Therapeutae, who affirmed 'At the beginning of each of my daily tasks, when I leave or enter the house, when I rise, when I stretch out on my couch, Him do I wish to celebrate'.

The Therapeutae were an Egyptian sect, described by the first-century Jewish scholar Philo, and believed to have been formed from the remnants of the Essene community who headed west from the Dead Sea after their dispersal following the fall of Jerusalem. Their attitude of constant prayerful attention is familiar to us today through the teaching of an even older tradition, Buddhism, and the practice of constant mindfulness that is at the root of Buddhist practice. It is this attitude which infused the saints of the Celtic church, who were teaching six hundred years after the Incarnation, and whose way of life, if not their doctrines, so closely resemble the precepts formulated by the Buddha six hundred years before the birth at Bethlehem. I am not suggesting that there was any direct historical link between Buddhism and the beliefs of the Celtic saints; although there were Buddhists in first century Alexandria, whose teachings were surely known to the Coptic church. It is certain, however that if we want to understand the depths of Celtic spirituality we shall find the nearest parallels in the Buddhist teaching of today as well as in the creation spirituality of such Christian teachers as Matthew Fox. Above all we will come close to Celtic thinking as, inspired by the obvious threats to the survival of our planet, we learn to be constantly mindful of the part we have to play in the divinity of the universe.

Cormac Mac Airt presiding at Tara

Beautiful was the appearance of Cormac in that assembly, flowing and slightly curling was his golden hair. A red buckler with stars and animals of gold and fastenings of silver upon him. A crimson cloak in wide descending folds around him, fastened at his neck with precious stones. A torque of gold around his neck. A white shirt with a full collar, and intertwined with red gold thread upon him. A girdle of gold, inlaid with precious stones, was around him. Two wonderful shoes of gold, with golden loops upon his feet. Two spears with golden sockets in his hands, with many rivets of red bronze. And he was himself, besides, symmetrical and beautiful of form, without blemish or reproach.

Version – Douglas Hyde

From 'The Instruction of King Cormac'

'O Cormac, grandson of Conn,' said Carbery,
'what were your habits when you were a lad?'
'Not hard to tell,' said Cormac.
'I was a listener in woods,
I was a gazer at stars,
I was blind where secrets were concerned,
I was silent in a wilderness,
I was talkative among many,
I was mild in the mead-hall,
I was stern in battle,
I was gentle towards allies,
I was a physician of the sick,
I was weak towards the feeble,
I was strong towards the powerful,
I was not close lest I should be burdensome,
I was not arrogant though I was wise,
I was not given to promising though I was strong,
I was not venturesome though I was swift,
I did not deride the old though I was young,
I was not boastful though I was a good fighter,
I would not speak about anyone in his absence,
I would not reproach, but I would give praise,
I would not ask, but I would give, –
for it is through these habits that the young
become old and kingly warriors.'

Early ninth-century, version – Kuno Meyer

Samhain

The Year's Beginning
The Coming of the Dark

 # Matthew

In the West, the feast of St Matthew, the evangelist, is celebrated on 21 September; but in the Eastern churches, with which the Celtic church had a close affinity through the connection with the Coptic tradition (*see* Introduction), his feast day comes on 16 November. It seems right that we should keep to that date, for whether he was martyred in Ethiopia, as the Roman martyrology claims, or in Persia according to St Jerome, he is clearly associated with North Africa and the Middle East. Moreover, his relics were said to have been brought to Finistère and to have been translated to Salerno in the Middle Ages. As we look through the lives of the Celtic saints in the course of the year, we shall see that many of them were to settle in Brittany; and although the worship of relics was not a part of their tradition, they must have shared the belief that the evangelist was enshrined in this corner of France.

At this time of year, when nature sleeps, we pause and consider our own humanity both as temporal and as eternal beings. So it is fitting that the symbol of the gospel writer for this season should not be a beast or a bird, but an image of mankind. In the *Book of Kells*, the figure who signifies Matthew is a winged and haloed being, carrying an elaborate cross, the arms of which meet to form a triple mandala, so echoing the triangular pattern of three red dots, a motif beloved by the Copts. The feathers on the wing-tips culminate in the same motif, which appears again in the portrait of the Matthew himself, for they decorate the cloak that he is wearing. The Coptic influence on the design is even more apparent in the carpet page, so called because of its resemblance to the weaving of a Persian carpet. Here the elaborate abstract designs take the form of a cross built up of eight circles, which also form a pattern slightly reminiscent of the Jewish kabbala.

The first version of this gospel, originally intended for Jewish Christians who still formed part of the congregation of the synagogues, makes that appropriate. At the start of his gospel,

Matthew traces the genealogy of Jesus back to Abraham, and time
and again he refers to the Old Testament books to prove that their
prophecies were fulfilled in Christ. Conversely he always seems
anxious to show that Jesus came to complete and not to destroy
the 'old law', giving up much of his report of the Sermon on the
Mount to an exposition of that law and to the affirmation that 'Till
Heaven and earth disappear, not one dot, not one little stroke, shall
disappear from the Law until its purpose is achieved'.

It is also surely appropriate that we should begin the Celtic
year with a gospel, which according to a tradition dating from
the second century, was the first to be written. That belief does
not refer to the Greek version of this testament, probably dating
from between 70 and 80 CE, but to an early Aramaic version, sadly
now lost.

It is also more than coincidence that the beginning of the Celtic
year comes at the start of winter, a few weeks later than the High
Holy Days with which the Jewish New Year begins. Both races
count time from the cycle of dark to light, and not as we do
from light to dark, beginning the day at sunrise and the year
with the return of the sun from the winter solstice. An even
more far-reaching connection is that both the tribal Jews and the
tribal Celts were a people necessarily rooted in the practical affairs
of life and aware of its hazards and dangers. For that reason both
the prayers of the modern Jewish prayer book and the traditional
prayers and verses of the Celtic people are inextricably bound
up with the daily routines of dressing, fire-lighting, cooking,
herding, working (in the fields and about the house), preparing
for a journey, and covering the fire at night.

Matthew's original Aramaic-speaking readers would have understood the point of the verses collected by Alexander Carmichael in
the Highlands of Scotland in the last century; while the story-loving
Celts, coming new to the gospel, must have found Matthew's
retelling of the parables entrancing. It is easy to imagine those
stories being related over and over again, with many embellish-
ments, by the glowing embers of the dying fire on the dark winter
evenings.

 # November

The Forces of the Dark

This is the thinnest time of the year, the season at which the veil between time and eternity can easily become transparent. It is now, when the darkness overtakes the light, that the Christian church chooses to celebrate the feasts of All Saints and All Souls; when we may say, in the words of Karl Rahner S.J. (translated by John M. Shea, and appearing in *The Eternal Year*, Burns and Oates, 1964), 'Be still, O heart, and let all whom you have loved rise from the grave of your breast.' The two worlds come together in that awareness of the spiritual beings, whom we may sense but cannot see with our physical eyes, and whose silence is of the same nature as the silence of God; more alive than much of our restless chatter. At this still time of the year, it often seems like a threat.

In the late Iron Age, when the Celtic tribes were beginning to adopt the Christian faith, Samhain was the time when the cattle which could not be over-wintered, had to be slaughtered. The bonfires, which we associate with this time of year, get their name from the 'bone fires', in which the inedible parts of the carcasses were destroyed. As for the feasting, which naturally went on at this time, when freshly killed meat was so abundant, the ancient laws of Ireland referred to it as 'winter food' in contrast to the dairy produce that was available in summer. This is a pattern that was laid down by the Neolithic farmers, some of whom drove their cattle up to the slaughter in the causewayed camp that stood on Windmill Hill long before the stones of Avebury were set in place beneath it.

No wonder then, that this season is associated with the malign forces of darkness and sorrow, as people awaited the coming of winter which was bound to bring death to so many, tragedies symbolized by the frantic lowing of the doomed beasts. The evening of All Hallows is a time when evil spirits can appear to triumph over the good. For the Celts, the elemental

demons were as real as the heavenly angels; and the immortal
light of the other world attracted the powers of darkness as
the nights lengthened and the trees shed their leaves in this
world.

Many Celtic prayers take the form of protective charms which
are designed to preserve the Christian soul from the forces of
darkness, as in this translation by N.D. O'Donoghue from some
lines of St Patrick's breastplate:

> God's shield to protect me,
> God's legions to save me
> from snares of the demons
> from evil enticements
> from failings of nature
> from one man or many
> that seek to destroy me
> anear or afar.

The Celts believed that everything we encounter each day needs
'saining' to drive out the lurking demons. There is a story told
of Columcille of Iona, who, as was his custom, blessed a pail of
milk brought to him by a young monk. When he did so, the milk
became turbulent and half of it spilled to the ground, for a demon
who lurked in the pail was disturbed by the saint's words. The evil
spirit had got there because the lad forgot to 'sain' the pail before
he started the milking.

The Jewish exorcists and the Welsh conjurors of the Middle Ages
were well aware of the need to cast out devils, and of the link between
sickness and demonic possession. Joan O'Grady in *The Prince of Darkness* (Element Books, 1989) points out that in Matthew's gospel, miracles of healing occur before the text of the Sermon on the Mount
is given. And as Thomas Chalmers concludes in his contribution to
An Introduction to Celtic Christianity edited by James P. Mackey (T.& T.
Clark, 1989), 'This good world is in bondage in the manner of a good
land under occupation by malevolent forces. However much the contemporary mind may feel like resisting the traditional Celtic personification of such forces, there can be no doubt that malevolent forces
operate in our world and through our own spirits and that we
need saving from them.'

The saints of the Celtic church whose feasts we celebrate this
month can give us such help, and guide us in our individual
struggles with the powers of darkness that attack us as the physical
light recedes.

GOTHIAN 1 November

In the nineteenth century, a Celtic oratory, 50 feet (15 m) long and 20 feet (6 m) wide, was excavated in the Cornish sands to the north-east of Hayle. The building is buried again now, but the church in the nearby village is dedicated to this Irish saint, who is thought to have landed here in the latter part of the sixth century and built his oratory on the coast. He is said to have been murdered by Teudor, a tyrannical local chieftain, soon after making his settlement.

By the late sixteenth century his name appears as Gwythyen and the first record of the modern spelling of Gwythian, by which the village is known, was in 1601.

Francis Kilvert, the diarist, was convinced that there was a Christian church here, coming direct from the East, before St Augustine came 'to bring us the Roman version of Christianity'; and on Friday 5 August 1870, while on holiday in Cornwall, he set out to to see 'the British Church buried in the sand'. He wrote that he and his companions 'came to the place suddenly and without warning and looked down into the church as into a long pit. The sand is drifted solid up to the very top of the outside walls. The walls are about four foot [1.2 m] high measured from the inside. So far they are almost perfect . . . The church is quite a small building, oblong, a door and window place still perceptible, and the faint remains of the rude pillars of a chancel arch still to be made out. Within the memory of persons still living the altar was standing, but the place has got into the hands of a dissenting farmer who keeps the place for a cattle yard and sheep fold and what more need be said.' At least the sands preserve it now.

CADFAN 1 November

Half-brother to the Breton Winwaloe (3 March) and a cousin of the Welsh Padarn (15 April), Cadfan spent time in both countries. He founded his main settlement at Tywyn on the coast between Dolgellau and Aberdovey, and his monastery flourished there at least until the thirteenth century, when a bard described Cadfan's church 'near the shore of the blue sea' as being a well-known place of sanctuary, as well as being famous for the many miracles that were wrought there. When Alban Butler's *Lives of the Saints* was revised in 1938, Cadfan's well by the church was 'enclosed within a stable'. It now lies in the grounds of the National Westminster Bank.

There is a tradition that Cadfan left Tywyn to sail across Cardigan Bay and become the first abbot of Bardsey Island at the end of the Lleyn Peninsula, a place so holy that the eighteenth-century Thomas Pennard tells us the local fisherman always 'made a full stop, pulled off their hats, and offered up a short prayer' as they approached it. That reverence may well have been tempered by fear of the swirling currents that divided this rock from the mainland.

In Brittany, Cadfan is taken as a patron of warriors, although it is not clear whether this suggests that he was a soldier before becoming a monk or a 'warrior from heaven'. Whatever the case, there is a statue of him dressed as a soldier and carrying a sword in a chapel near Juimpier.

Although he probably died on Bardsey Island, he was buried at Tywyn, where an ancient inscribed stone, now preserved in the church, bears the memorial to Cadfan in Old Welsh and is said to have once marked the place of his burial.

Blessing

> Be each saint in heaven,
> Each sainted woman in heaven,
> Each angel in heaven
> Stretching their arms for you,
> Smoothing the way for you,
> When you go thither
>   Over the river hard to see;
> Oh when you go thither home
>   Over the river hard to see.

Collected by Alexander Carmichael

CLYDOG   3 November

Clodock on the banks of the River Monnow, on the borders between England and Wales in the Black Mountains, got its name because it was at this place that the oxen drawing the body of this murdered, saintly king refused to be driven further when the yoke broke as they were about to go through the ford. Born into the

family of Brychan (6 April), Clydog ruled the area of Ewyas with
peace and justice, until he was treacherously killed while hunting,
by a jealous comrade. Many miracles were said to have taken place
at his tomb.

WINEFRIDE   3 November

A niece of Beuno (21 April), being his sister's daughter, Winefride
became his disciple when he visited her family, and set up a church
in the area of north-east Wales where she lived. While he was there,
a local chieftain, who had long wanted to marry the girl, became
so furious at her constant refusal that one June day he slashed at
her with his sword and cut off her head as she sought refuge in
the church that Beuno had built.

In the middle of the twelfth century, Robert of Shrewsbury
wrote a life of Winefride in which he tells us that immediately
the evil deed was done the ground opened up to to swallow her
murderer, while from the place where the girl's head fell a stream
burst out of the rock. Furthermore, Beuno restored her to life,
setting her head back on her shoulders, so that only a tiny scar
remained.

Winefride lived for a further fifteen years, having entered a
nunnery at Gwytherin after her miraculous resuscitation. She was
the abbess when she died. The spring that flowed at her beheading
became the shrine of Holywell, a place that today draws thousands
of pilgrims each year, as it has done for centuries. William Caxton's
printed life of the saint claims that the well, 'largely endurying to
this day, which heleth al langours and sekenesses as well in men
as in bestes'; and on 3 August 1774, Samuel Johnson saw people
bathing in its waters. The buildings enclosing the well were set
up at the command and expense of Margaret, mother of Henry
VII (1457–1509).

KEA   5 November

Possibly a cousin of Beuno (21 April), Kea, like many other
Welsh monks journeyed to Brittany through Britain's south-west
peninsula, spending long stretches of time in Cornwall, Devon
and Somerset. It is in the latter county that he is particularly
remembered, for although places elsewhere still bear his name

and that of his travelling companion Rumon (I think particularly of Landkey – the church of Kea – and the nearby Romansley – the field of Rumon – to the south of Barnstaple), it is from Somerset that we have the fullest accounts of these men.

They both came, in the sixth century, to the wattle church at Glastonbury, when Gildas (29 January) was living as a hermit on one of the islands rising from the shallow sea to the north-west, in the same area as Street, established as a causeway across the marshes of the Brue. Here at Leigh (recorded in a document of 725 as Lantokai, the church of Kea) where the land climbs up to the ridge of Ivy Thorn, Kea had his own hermitage, cherishing a prayer bell that Gildas is said to have made for him.

Legend links both Gildas and Kea with the Arthurian story, claiming that the latter attempted to restore peace between Arthur and Mordred, and persuaded Guinevere to enter a nunnery.

When he eventually arrived in Brittany, where he is remembered as St Quay, he founded a monastery at Cleder, 5 miles (8 km) to the west of St Pol de Leon. In Breton images of the saint he is frequently connected with a stag. His name was invoked as a cure for toothache.

MELAINE　6 November

Patron of Mullion on the Lizard peninsula in Cornwall, Melaine, who died in the middle of the sixth century, is primarily remembered as an authoritarian Bishop of Rennes who wanted to conform to Roman practices. It was he who demanded that the Breton priests should cease from 'wandering from cabin to cabin celebrating Mass on portable altars, accompanied by women who administered the chalice to the faithful'.

ILLTYD　6 November

Illtyd, who lived at the end of the fifth century, was one of the most illustrious of the Welsh teachers and had David (1 March) as pupil. He is said to have spent some time at the monastic community founded by Cassian near Marseilles and to have been ordained by Germanus of Auxerre (31 July). Most accounts agree that he started out as a soldier, and that he was a married man. His wife is referred to in the lives of the saint as Trinihid, a name which

Illtyd

St Illtyd's Church, Caldey

is built into Llanrhidian on Gower and Llantrihyd in Glamorgan, some 8 miles (13 km) north-east of Illtyd's collegiate monastery at the place marked on Ordinance Survey maps as Llantwit Major. In Welsh it is called Llanilltud Fawr, the great settlement of Illtyd. It stands by the river Hoddnant.

According to a Norman clerk who wrote from that place, Illtyd's name comes from the Latin '*Ille ab omni crimine tutus*' ('the one safe from all evil'). The Welsh tradition, based on an early life of Cadoc (25 September), describes Illtyd's conversion as taking place when fifty soldiers under his command were swallowed into the earth. Another tradition tells us that his conversion took place after a hunting accident in which several of his friends were killed and that it was Dyfrig (14 November) who was responsible for bringing Illtyd into the church.

In the life of Cadoc, it is that saint who granted Illtyd's request to be given the monastic habit and tonsure. As soon as he had become a monk an angel spoke to him, saying 'When thou shalt arise tomorrow, hasten towards a certain wooded valley to the west, where you shall have an abode. For so is the will of God, seeing that the place is convenient, very fertile and suitable for human habitation.' So Illtyd went to the valley, and only when he had settled in that place 'well watered by a number of springs, from which flow brooks running into the pretty river that drains it' did he go to make confession to Dyfrig, then Bishop of Llandaff, and receive from him the plans for his monastery.

As well as the young David, Samson (28 July), Gildas (29 January) and Paul Aurelian (12 March) were all attracted to Illtyd's collegiate church. The Breton monk Wrmonoc, who wrote a life of the last-named saint, tells us of the miracle that happened when Illtyd asked those four to pray with him that his monastic lands might be extended. After they had prayed, 'accompanied by his disciples, he went down to the shore at low tide, where the sea used to withdraw to the distance of a mile or more, and traced with the point of his staff a furrow, beyond which he forbade the water to pass, and it has never since that time transgressed his command'. Moreover the reclaimed land proved very fertile, producing an abundance of crops for the monastery.

Like many other Celtic abbots, Illtyd withdrew from time to time from his monastery, seeking out a cave by the banks of the Ewenny River, sleeping each night on a cold stone and keeping himself alive by heaven-sent offerings of barley loaves and fish.

He is also said to have had a retreat at Llanhamlach, 3 miles (5 km) to the east of Brecon where, according to the twelfth-century Giraldus Cambrensis, 'the mare that used to carry his provisions to him was covered by a stag, and produced an animal of wonderful speed, resembling a horse before and a stag behind'.

The Welsh belief is that Illtyd was in fact born near Brecon, and that he was buried on the high moor that now bears the name of Mynydd Illtyd and has been chosen for the site of the National Park's Mountain Centre. Other sources tell us that he was born in Brittany and that he returned there to die. He is invoked in a Salisbury psalter of Breton origin and a hymn was sung in his honour at the procession which took place during the pardon of Tréquier. The Breton pardons, days of religious observance which take place on the feast days of local saints, probably originated in the Middle Ages, but many of the saints who are celebrated came into Brittany from Ireland and Wales in the fifth and sixth centuries.

Some of the marvellous stories recounted of Illtyd connect him with the court of King Arthur. Together with Cadoc he is said to have been one of the guardians of the Holy Grail, and a late eleventh-century life claims that he was Arthur's cousin and served as one of his knights. On Gower, where the little church at Oxwich is dedicated to him, he is connected with one version of the death of Arthur. The eighth-century Nennius in his *Marvels of Britain* tells us that while Illtyd 'was praying in a cave near the sea, a boat came in which were two men and the body of a holy man, an altar floating above his face. When Illtyd went forth to meet them, they took out of the ship the body of the holy man, the altar still stood suspended and never moved from its position. Then the men in the boat said to Illtyd "This man of God charged us to bring him to thee and to bury him with thee, and that thou shouldst not reveal his name to anyone for fear lest men should swear by him".' The dead man, whom nobody was to 'swear by' – taking vows at his tomb – was, of course, the 'once and future king'.

What would Illtyd himself have made of such a story? In a life of Samson written at Dol about a hundred years after Illtyd's death, he is described as 'the most learned of all the Britons in the knowledge of scripture, both the Old Testament and the New Testament, and in every branch of philosophy – poetry and rhetoric, grammar and arithmetic; and he was most sagacious and gifted with the power of telling future events'.

The Coming of Winter

I have news for you; the stag bells, winter snows, summer has gone.
Wind high and cold, the sun low, short its course, the sea running
  high.
Deep red the bracken, its shape is lost; the wild goose has raised its
  accustomed cry.
Cold has seized the birds' wings; season of ice, this is my news.

Irish, ninth-century, author unknown

CYBI   8 November

Great-grandson of Geraint, King of Cornwall, Cybi is honoured
at Duloe near Liskeard and at Tregony. An unreliable thirteenth-
century life tells us that he could read at the age of seven (a
remarkable event in the sixth century) and that when he was
twenty-seven he made a pilgrimage to Jerusalem.

On becoming a monk, he travelled north, crossing the Channel
to Wales (a reversal of the usual pattern) and settled by the Usk,
at the place now called Llangybi. Later he went west to Menevia,
the area around St David's on the north Pembrokeshire coast.
To reach that place, he probably travelled along the Golden
Road, the ridgeway track across the Preseli Hills, which got
its name from its use by prehistoric traders heading towards the
Wicklow Hills.

Like them, Cybi was destined to set sail for Ireland where he
spent four years on the Arran island of Inishmore with Enda
(21 March). The story goes that he fell into a dispute there,
and returned to Wales, crossing the Irish Sea in a coracle whose
frame had no covering hides.

With his friend, Seriol (1 February), he eventually landed in
Anglesey, the island that was to become the centre of his cult.
There he made his settlement at Holyhead on the site of a Roman
fort, subsequently known as Caer Gybi.

There are several other dedications to him in Wales. You will
find a Llangybi in the Teifi Valley and another near Pwllheli on
Lleyn. Near to the latter there are the remains of a beehive cell, set
in a valley on the edge of a wood about a quarter of a mile from
the parish church. St Cybi's well nearby is still used for baptism
and healing.

TYSILIO   8 November

Born at Shrewsbury, at the palace of Pengwern, into the royal family of Powys at the end of the sixth century, Tysilio, while still a young man ran away to become a monk against his father's wishes. For seven years he was forced to take refuge on an island in the Menai Straits. At the end of that time he deemed it safe to return to his old teacher, Gwyddfarch, at the monastery of Meifod. Eventually he became abbot there.

As the years went by the roles were reversed and Tysilio became Gwyddfarch's teacher. When the old man wanted to make a pilgrimage to Rome, the young abbot told him that what he really wanted was to see the great buildings there, and advised him to dream about them instead. Then he took Gwyddfarch for a long walk over the mountains of Snowdonia, not failing to point out to him that the journey to Rome would be infinitely more exhausting. Worn out, the aged monk slept deeply, and did indeed see all the glories of the Holy City in his dreams. He was satisfied and stayed at home.

In 617, the Saxon victory at the Battle of Chester led to the massacre of the monks at Bangor, and the royal court of Powys withdrew from Shrewsbury to Mathrafae near Merford. This disturbed Tysilio greatly, for he did not want to be drawn into political machinations. So he went south, first to Builth, and then left Wales for Brittany. There he settled at a place now called Saint Sullac, the Breton version of his name. He was to die there in 640, after he had sent his crozier (a staff based on a long-shafted cross) and gospel book (a transcription from the Evangelists) back to Wales as a sign of his blessing.

AEDH MAC BRIC   10 November

Although he was born into the royal Ulster family of Niall of the Nine Hostages (see page 3), as a youth Aedh was employed as his father's swineherd. When some pigs went astray, Brendan of Birr (29 November) and Kenneth (Canice, 11 October) helped him to find them.

On his father's death, Aedh's brothers denied him his share of his inheritance, and so he sought refuge in Offaly where he became a monk. He went on to found his own churches in West Meath.

There are three Latin lives of the saint recording the many miracles he accomplished. He is said to have been skilled in medicine and to have relieved Brigid of a constant headache. When the pain lifted a gospel book miraculously appeared on her lap, and she handed it to Aedh.

When Aedh came to die, Columcille (9 June) on Iona was aware of the instant of the holy man's death. A ruined hermitage where Aedh is said to have meditated stands at Slieve League, and is still the goal of an annual pilgrimage.

MARTIN OF TOURS 11 November

Born in Pannonia (now Hungary), the son of an officer in the Roman army, Martin, a Magyar who became Bishop of Tours in 572, has a place in the Celtic calendar for two reasons. The first is that he was the pioneer of Western monasticism, providing the model for the Christian settlements and colleges established in Ireland, Scotland and Wales from the fifth century; and the second, no less important, is that he was one of the first leaders of the church to take the gospels out from the towns and cities to small isolated communities living in the moors, on the mountains, and on off-shore islands.

It is ironic that Martin's feast should fall on the day on which we remember the fallen of two world wars; for he would not be made whole-heartedly welcome at military cenotaph ceremonies. Having followed his father's profession and started his career as a soldier, he was imprisoned by the Roman authorities after his conversion to Christianity, when he realized that his beliefs were in no way compatible with his duties as a soldier.

After he became ordained, he journeyed into Gaul and eventually established his monastery, the first in western Europe, at Marmoutier. There, following the Egyptian model, he lived for much of his time as a hermit, apart from the monastic community, in a cliff cave. It is claimed that Ninian (26 August) visited him there; and that on returning to his native Britain, modelled his own church and collegiate monastery on Martin's foundation in Gaul. In dedicating his white stone church (Candida Casa) on the Solway Firth to Martin, Ninian was setting a precedent for church dedications throughout Britain. In nearly all cases a church bearing Martin's name denotes the site of the earliest Christian community in any neighbourhood. Bede reminds us that the ancient church of St Martin, outside the east walls of Canterbury, well predates the cathedral, having been built, he claims, during the Roman occupation.

By the end of the fifth century, manuscripts of the life of Martin were to be found in the monastic libraries of Ireland; and his festival was celebrated with such enthusiasm that in 578 the Synod of Auxerre forbade feasting on the eve of Martinmas, which was said to have turned into a drunken orgy. No doubt the celebrations connected with Martin became linked with the feasts of Samhain; and by the Middle Ages the saint had become the patron of blacksmiths, most probably because of the association with the fire festivals of this time of year. The other explanation is that the smiths adopted him because he is usually portrayed on horseback, leaning out of the saddle to divide his cloak with a beggar. That episode comes from the famous story of Martin's conversion, which tells how he clothed a nearly naked beggar at Amiens whom he encountered while on cavalry duty. The next night he is said to have dreamt that Christ approached him wearing the cloak which he had given away. It was after that vision that he was baptized.

CADWALADER   12 November

A Welsh king and son of Cadwallon, who as an ally of Penda of Mercia, defeated and killed Edwin, King of Northumbria, in 633. Cadwalader was such a peace-loving prince that he earned the nickname of the battle-shunner. However in 658 he was forced to lead his people against a Saxon army in Somerset. He was defeated.

MACHAR (MOCHUNNA)   12 November

In 563, Machar came to Iona with Columcille (9 June). He preached throughout the island of Mull, and then travelled east to evangelize the Picts around Aberdeen, where water from his well was, at one time, used for baptisms in the cathedral.

Encompassing

The holy Apostles' guarding,
The gentle martyrs' guarding,
The nine angels' guarding,
     Be cherishing me, be aiding me.

The quiet Brigid's guarding,
The gentle Mary's guarding,
The warrior Michael's guarding,
     Be shielding me, be aiding me.

The God of the elements' guarding,
The loving Christ's guarding,
The Holy Spirit's guarding,
     Be cherishing me, be aiding me.

Collected by Alexander Carmichael

Rune of Hospitality

I saw a stranger yestreen;
I put food in the eating place,
Drink in the drinking place,
Music in the listening place;
And, in the sacred name of the Triune,
He blessed myself and my house,
My cattle and my dear ones.
And the lark said in her song,
     Often, often, often,
Goes the Christ in the stranger's guise:
     Often, often, often,
Goes the Christ in the stranger's guise.

Traditional

DYFRIG (DUBRICIUS)   14 November

The legend is that Dyfrig was the son of a princess, whose father
was so angry at her pregnancy that he ordered her to be thrown
into the Wye. The river refused to drown her, floating her first
to one shore and then to the other. Frustrated, her furious father
ordered her burning. Her executioners left her tied to a stake above

the faggots, but the next day when they returned they found her alive, the baby at her breast. The child was brought to the king, and there performed his first miracle when he cured his grandfather of some form of leprosy.

This story had its foundation in the saint's link with the Wye Valley and his relationship with the tribal leaders who gave him land to found monasteries at Madley, Hentland (4 miles (6 km) to the north of Ross-on-Wye, near Archenfield and based on the Roman city of Ariconum) and Moccas (the place of the pigs). The latter was so called because in response to an angelic vision, Dyfrig built a church dedicated to the Holy Trinity there, at the place where he found a white sow with her litter.

Dyfrig is said to have been a pupil of Germanus of Auxerre (31 July), but we must understand by this that he followed that prelate's teaching, for the two men are divided by a century of time. However, he certainly seems to have taken a strong stance against the Pelagian heresy of the supremacy of the will, and to have persuaded his friend David (1 March) to preach against it at the Synod of Llanddewi Brefi. He is also said to have spent some time with Teilo (9 February) at Llandeilo Fawr.

A life of Samson (28 July) informs us that Dyfrig was at one time Abbot of Caldey Island; and the more than unreliable Geoffrey of Monmouth claims that as Archbishop of Caerleon he presided at Silchester at the coronation of the fifteen-year-old Arthur, a theme later taken up by Tennyson.

In the middle of the sixth century, Samson's biographer tells us that Dyfrig 'oppressed by certain infirmities and by old age, resigned the laborious task of the episcopal office, and resuming the eremetical life, in company with several holy men and their disciples, who lived by the labour of their hands, he dwelt alone for many years on the island of Bardsey and gloriously finished his life there'. In the twelfth century his relics were taken to Llandaff, being taken to the mainland of the Lleyn Peninsula on 7 May 1120 and finally reaching the cathedral of South Wales on Sunday 23 May. There his head and one arm were encased in silver reliquaries and drew hundreds of pilgrims until the middle of the sixteenth century.

HILDA   17 November

A Saxon, related to the royal families of East Anglia and Northumberland and born in 614, Hilda was to become a staunch advocate and practioner of what Bede described as 'the primitive church' of the Celts. He also tells us that when Hilda was a little girl, when her parents were living in exile in Elmet (now Yorkshire) under the protection of the Celtic Cedric, her mother Bregusuith, dreaming that her husband was to be taken away from her (he was, in-fact, shortly thereafter to be poisoned), searched everywhere for him. 'When all her efforts had failed, she discovered a most valuable jewel under her garments; and as she looked closely, it emitted such a brilliant light that all Britain was lit by its splendour.' This dream, Bede concludes, 'was fulfilled in her daughter, whose life afforded a shining example not only to her herself but to all who wished to live a good life'.

With her great-uncle Edwin, King of Northumbria, Hilda, as a very young woman, heard Paulinus preach. He was one of the monks sent by Pope Gregory the Great to evangelize England. As a result of that experience she was baptized, either at Easter in 628 in the wooden church at York, or later that year in the waters of the River Swale where it flowed past the site of the royal palace at Yeavering. For nearly twenty years after that, until she was thirty-three, she lived the life of a high-ranking lady, remaining unmarried and presumably dwelling with her mother.

Although she had become a Christian through the words of an emissary from Rome, it was the teaching of Aidan (31 August) at Lindisfarne that was to have the greatest effect on her. For when she decided to become a nun, it was he who instructed her, eventually giving her a small plot of land on the banks of the Wear as a place to live out her vocation.

From there she went to join the community at Hartlepool, and eventually became its abbess, establishing a rule based on the Irish church and the teachings of Columbanus (21 November). Then in 657, she founded her own double monastery for men and women at Streanaeshalch, the place we now know as Whitby. There, according to Bede, 'She established the same regular life as in her former monastery, and taught the observance of righteousness, mercy, purity, and other virtues, but especially of peace and charity . . . So great was her prudence that not only ordinary folk, but kings and princes used to come to ask her advice in their difficulties and take it. Those under her direction were required to make a thorough study of the Scriptures and occupy themselves in good works to such good effect that many were found fitted for Holy Orders and the service of God's altar.' We know that she also found time to encourage the most humble people to find their true vocation; and that even her cowherd, the stammering lay-brother Caedmon, found his voice as he worked for her, and came to compose the forceful hymn glorifying the God of creation.

Together with Cuthbert (20 March), Hilda worked tirelessly to try to find a resolution to the disputes arising from the differing doctrines of the Roman and Celtic wings of the church; even to the extent of offering her own abbey as the place where the disputants could meet to discuss their case in the presence of the King of Northumbria. The result of that Synod of Whitby in 664 was to alter the course of church history in these islands, imposing an urban, foreign and quaesi-military hierarchy as the established church took on the role of the vanished Roman empire.

Ten years after the stress and disappointment of that Synod, Hilda was taken ill with a burning fever, which Bede tells us 'racked her continually for six years'. At dawn on 17 November in the seventh year she received the Last Sacrament and having summoned her nuns around her and urged them to maintain the peace of the gospel, she died.

That night, in a monastery that she had established at Hackness, thirteen miles away, the nun Begu had a vision in which she saw Hilda's soul being born up to Heaven guided by angels.

About a hundred years after Hilda's death, Whitby was sacked by the Danes, which casts some doubt on the allegation that Hilda's relics were brought to Glastonbury in the tenth century, especially as Gloucester makes the same claim. There is no doubt however of the importance of the cult of this wise and generous woman throughout England during the Middle Ages. Hilda was an encourager, and enabler. As we have seen it was through her insistence that the stuttering, illiterate Caedmon (11 February), a monk in her monastery, came to write the great Anglo-Saxon poem of the creation. People still take heart from Hilda's example, and in 1986 a group of women, mostly Anglican with Monica Furlong as their spokesperson, formed the St Hilda Community. *Women Included: The St Hilda Community* (SPCK, 1991) gives the origin of that community and presents the liturgies and prayers that have grown out of it.

Collect for Hilda's Day

O God our vision,
in our mother's womb
you formed us for your glory.
As your servant Hilda
shone like a jewel in the church
may we now delight to claim her gifts
of judgement and inspiration
reflected in the women of this age.

Women Included: The St Hilda Community

MAWES   18 November

In Cornish tradition, Mawes is the founder and patron of the
fishing village near Falmouth that bears his name. However it is
in Brittany that he is best known, and where he became a bishop.
He made his settlement on the island of Modez near the coast of
Leon in the gulf of St Brieuc. There he gained a reputation as both
a teacher and a healer. He was popularly invoked to cure headaches,
worms and snake bites.

About sixty churches and chapels in Brittany are dedicated to
him, and his relics are venerated at Juimpier, Treguier, Lesnevin
and Bourges.

I Lie Down this Night

I lie down this night with God,
    And God will lie down with me;
I lie down this night with Christ,
    And Christ will lie down with me;
I lie down this night with Spirit,
    And the Spirit will lie down with me;
God and Christ and the Spirit
    Be lying down with me.

Collected by Alexander Carmichael

COLUMBANUS   21 November

Born in 543 to a noble Leinster family in the area between Wexford and Carlow, Columbanus was to become probably the first and certainly one of the most influential of the Irish missionaries to the continent. It was a woman hermit who led him to his vocation as a monk.

His first teacher was a disciple of Finnian of Moville (10 September). Later he went to Bangor, choosing to follow the austere regime imposed by Comgall (11 May), whose disciple he became. There he learned Latin and Greek. At the late age of fifty-seven, he set out with twelve companions for Gaul. His first church was set on the site of a ruined temple of Diana in the Vosges, and from there he went on to establish a second Christian settlement in another Roman ruin: a discarded hill fort at Luxeuil, destroyed by Attila in 451.

He might have made his final settlement there had he not angered King Theodric II by refusing to bless his illegitimate sons. For that act of intransigence, Columbanus was ordered to be deported to Ireland and taken under military escort to Nantes. The ship on which he set out was, however, forced back by a storm and Columbanus, hoping to find refuge, travelled to Metz. There he met some of his own monks from Luxeuil, who rowed him up the Rhine, with the intention that he might make a new settlement on the shores of Lake Constance at Brequez. When they landed there they found the people so hostile that they were forced back into their boat and so crossed the water. That is how, in 613, at the age of seventy, Columbanus came to found his most famous monastery at Bobbio in the Appennines. Once again, he built on a site that had known a religious use – but this time it was a ruined church which served as the foundation for his monastery.

In all his settlements Columbanus inaugurated a rule that conformed strictly to the Irish tradition. In doing so he calculated the date of Easter according to the Celtic manner (writing to Pope Gregory the Great on the subject) and incurring the anger of the Archbishop of Lyons by insisting that an abbot had the ultimate authority over his monastery.

His own rule was built on a regime of silence, prayer and fasting, eating only an evening meal of porridge, vegetables, beans and bread. More severe fasting was imposed for a penance: anyone of his community who stole a domestic animal had to live on bread and water for 120 days. For the wider community and for the lay brothers, the penances were tailored to the fault; from the talkative he demanded silence; from the restless, gentleness; and the greedy were told to fast.

As well as composing a rule and penitentiary for posterity, he also left us a handful of poems, including a boating song. His affinity with animals was so complete that he could charm the squirrels out of the trees. He was only in Bobbio for two years before he died on 23 November 615, the day on which his feast is kept in Ireland. Three years after he died, the monk Jonas came to Bobbio, and wrote a life of the monastery's founder based on conversations with those who had known him.

COLMAN OF CLOYNE 24 November

Throughout the latter part of the sixth century, Colman was the royally appointed bard at the palace of Cashel. It was there, according to tradition, that Brendan (16 May) discovered the relics of Ailbe (12 September); an event which so impressed the fifty-year-old Colman that he became a Christian. Subsequently he became ordained and went on to become a bishop, working in Limerick and Cork.

Going to Rest

May the Light of lights come
    To my dark heart from Thy place;
    May the Spirit's wisdom come
    To my heart's tablet from my Saviour.

Be the peace of the Spirit mine this night,
Be the peace of the Son mine this night,
Be the peace of the Father mine this night,
    The peace of all peace be mine this night,
Each morning and evening of my life.

Collected by Alexander Carmichael

VIRGIL (FERGHILL)   27 November

This eighth-century Irish monk, who was probably a disciple of Samthann (18 December), is said to have brought the relics of Brigid (1 February) to Salzburg, where he became bishop. Because he postulated a cosmology in which another fairy world, with its own sun and moon, existed beneath this one, he was condemned for heretical teaching by the fundamentalist, Saxon evangelist Boniface of Crediton, whose mission was to stamp out pagan practices on the Continent.

CONGAR   27 November

At Lanivet in mid-Cornwall, 2 miles (3 km) south of Bodmin, there is a farm called St Ingonger, with a holy well and a chapel dedicated to this sixth-century evangelist of the south-west peninsula. In Somerset, he is particularly associated with Congresbury on the northern slopes of the Mendip Hills. His monastery there is mentioned in Bishop Asser's life of King Alfred, and from the beginning of the eleventh century the church at Congresbury claimed to have the body of the saint, who was also honoured at Dunster Priory and at Muchelney Abbey near Langport, where this day ranked as one of the principal feasts.

FERGUS   27 November

Known as 'the Pict' in his native Ireland, Fergus, who lived in the eighth century, became a bishop in eastern Scotland, where he founded many churches. A well and a cave at Glamis are both associated with him, and it is there that he died. His relics were honoured in that place until the late fifteenth century.

JUTHWARA   28 November

Like her sister, Sidwell of Exeter (2 August), Juthwara was the victim of a jealous step-mother who incited her son Bana to murder her, by making out that Juthwara was pregnant. Fooled by that deceit, he became so furious that he slashed the girl's head off, whereupon a spring of water gushed from the rock where it fell. Immediately the headless virgin picked up her severed head and carried it to the church.

That story is said to relate to the Cornish village of Lanteglos near Camelford; and the two sisters are shown on the rood screens in the Devon churches of Hennock and Ashton. A Breton statue of Juthwara shows her holding her head in her hands.

BRENDAN OF BIRR 29 November

A friend and disciple of Columcille (9 June), Brendan of Birr was known as the chief of the prophets of Ireland. Through his intervention at the Synod of Meltown in Meath, the order of excommunication on Columcille was rescinded. The two men were so close that Columcille on Iona was aware of Brendan's death in the west of Ireland and saw the angels carrying his soul to heaven.

Scel Lem Duib

Here's a song –
stags give tongue
winter snows
summer goes.

High cold blow
sun is low
brief his day
seas give spray.

Fern clumps redden
shapes are hidden
wildgeese raise
wonted cries.

Cold now girds
wings of birds
icy time –
that's my rime.

Ninth-century, version – Flann O'Brien

NOVEMBER PILGRIMAGE

Monastic Site, Tywyn Cadfan

November is a good time to visit Tywyn, for by now all the holiday visitors will have gone, and the daylight hours are just long enough to follow the pilgrim route, which was also an old drove road, across the hills to the site of Cadfan's monastery. Long before the saint settled on this coast, the Romans came this way, so you will be walking on the path of legionaries, medieval pilgrims and eighteenth-century cattle dealers.

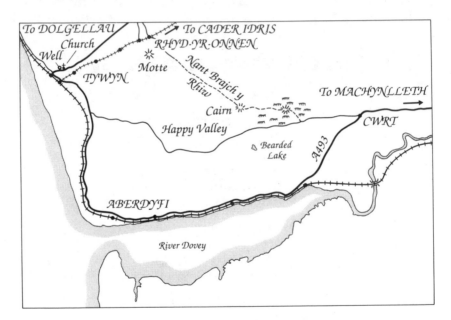

To reach the old track, take the A493 from Machynlleth to Aberdyfi and leave the main road at Cwrt, where you will see a signpost to the Happy Valley. Follow that lane for about a mile (1½ km) until, at the foot of a steep climb, you will notice a stony path to your right, winding its way over some rocky outcrops. Once clear of the rocks you will come to a cairn and from that point the old track goes straight to the north-west for some 3 miles (5 km) to bring you into the village of Rhyd-yr-Onnen. Here you will find the railway line, and because this now only serves a holiday steam train, you can walk along the track to the church in Tywyn, which houses the stone which bears the memorial to Cadfan in Old Welsh, and is said to have once marked the place of his burial.

The weather in November can obviously be treacherous, so if you undertake this walk, dress sensibly, wear boots if possible, take some food with you, and make sure that somebody locally knows of your undertaking. If you are driving, it is still good to come to this locality in November when you can have the lanes to yourself and make your way from Tywyn to the Cader Idris range.

 # December

The Winter Solstice

In the third millennium BC, the people who cultivated the fertile valley of the Boyne to the west of Dublin built elaborate passage graves for the bones of their dead. One such funeral barrow at New Grange has been carefully excavated and restored to reveal stone slabs, carved with intricate swirling designs. They stand at the entranceway and line the inner chamber, which is reached through a narrow passage, so designed that it makes an abrupt change of direction before reaching the inner sanctum where the bones of the bodies, burnt on the funeral pyres by the river, were stored. The whole edifice is so aligned that the rays of the solstice sunrise are deflected through that passage, so that at dawn on that day of the year, if the skies are clear, the whole chamber, plunged in darkness at all other times, receives the light.

By the time the Iron Age Celts had settled in the Boyne Valley and round the other places known to the earliest inhabitants of Ireland, the ancient burial mounds were grassed over. They had become places to be regarded with awe and dread, and as the *sidh*, a word denoting a magical dwelling place, they were the home of fairy creatures, described in the myths as fierce and horrible, and in no way to be confused with the gossamer sylphs of Victorian fancy. The fear of the *sidh* was compounded when the iron-working smiths followed their craft near the old barrows, for they were not allowed to settle near the tribe they served.

In order to have sufficient heat for their work, the smiths set their fires in dark places, where they would burn most brightly. In the Middle Ages smithcraft was to be associated with alchemy; and to the Celts the work was thought to be a manifestation of the other world, which the *sidh*-dwellers also inhabited. Although the name of Wayland smithy comes from the elfin metalworker of Norse mythology, it is not for nothing that the long barrow on the Ridgeway above the Vale of the White Horse should be so-called.

As the smiths worked by the old barrows, performing their own magic of shaping the metal on which the whole culture depended and causing the sparks to fly out of dark caverns, it is no wonder that the newly formed Christian tribes felt that these were places where darkness fought against the light, and where demons were present.

The battle, as they were well aware, took place in the minds of men, and it raged particularly fiercely for those who had chosen to live alone in remote hermitages: sea caves, huts by mountain streams and in thick forests. There the hermit monks of the early church prayed through the dark months. In *Station Island*, the poet, Seamus Heaney, describes such a monk, ruthlessly cutting himself off from the world, so that like the bones at New Grange and buried iron, his contemplation could revitalize the earth:

> As he prowled the rim of his clearing
> where the blade of choice had not spared
> one stump of affection
> he was like a ploughshare
> interred to sustain the whole field
> of force.

Many leaders of the Celtic church, who chose to spend so much time as solitaries, came together with their families, friends and fellow Christians for a short while at this time of year. It is a tradition that the most secular of us still follow, as we observe or run away from the family gatherings of Christmas and New Year. For this time of the return of the light, and the promise of the rebirth of the sun, soon became associated with the nativity of Christ. That festival was less central to the early church than the Resurrection of Easter, but in northern latitudes especially it was linked with the celebrations that greeted the intimations of returning light and warmth, although winter still had so much of its course to run.

In the Eastern Orthodox church, Christmas is celebrated on 6 January, when we, in the West, are keeping Epiphany. It seems possible that this was the time for the Celtic Christmas, for it marks the end of the plateau of the solstice and the time when the days perceptibly begin to lengthen.

TUDWAL   1 December

On St Tudwal's island off the south coast of the Lleyn Peninsula, there is a ruined chapel which is said to have been the saint's hermitage. However Tudwal is mainly honoured in Brittany, especially in the area around Leon. He lived during the sixth century.

Bless to me, O God

> Bless to me, O God,
>   Each thing mine eye sees;
> Bless to me, O God,
>   Each sound mine ear hears;
> Bless to me, O God,
>   Each odour that goes to my nostrils;
> Bless to me, O God,
>   Each taste that goes to my lips;
>   Each note that goes to my song,
>   Each ray that guides my way,
>   Each thing that I pursue,
>   Each lure that tempts my will,
>   The zeal that seeks my living soul,
> The Three that seek my heart,
>   The zeal that seeks my living soul,
> The Three that seek my heart.

Collected by Alexander Carmichael

I am Bending my Knee

> I am bending my knee
> In the eye of the Father who created me,
> In the eye of the Son who purchased me,
> In the eye of the Spirit who cleansed me,
>   In friendship and affection.
> Through Thine own Anointed One, O God,
> Bestow upon us fullness in our need.

Collected by Alexander Carmichael

JUSTINIAN   5 December

Born in Brittany in the sixth century, Justinian reversed the usual direction of travelling priests by coming north to Wales, where he made his hermitage on Ramsey Island off the Pembrokeshire coast. When he first arrived there, he found the island inhabited by another devout man, Honarius, living with his sister and her maid. Justinian demanded that the women be sent to the mainland, and the two men settled down amicably together, befriended by David, whose wild territory of Menevia is just across the water from Ramsey.

The friendship between David and Justinian became so close that Justinian had no hesitation in taking a boat across the sound to the mainland when he heard that David was ill. In fact, the story goes, the sailors who rowed him across were devils in disguise and the tales they had told him were false, for David was in perfect health. On that occasion the saint realized what was happening and escaped the snares of his would-be murderers. However, the devils attacked again, this time inciting Justinian's three servants to become so enraged when their master told them to work harder that they threw Justinian to the ground and cut off his head. As we have come to expect, a spring of healing water gushed forth from the place where the saint's head struck the ground. As for the servants, they were inflicted with leprosy and lived out the remainder of their days on a lonely crag.

There is a chapel devoted to Justinian by the lifeboat station at Porthstinian across the water from Ramsey, and a church dedicated to him at Llanstinian near Fishguard. His shrine still stands in St David's Cathedral.

DIUMA   7 December

When Peada, son of Penda, the pagan king of Mercia, was baptized in 652, Fintan (17 February), Bishop of Lindisfarne, sent four priests to that kingdom. The Irish Diuma was one of that number, Cedd, brother of Chad (2 March) was another. After Penda's death in 654, Diuma was consecrated Bishop of Mercia.

BUDOC 8 December

Grandson of the King of Brest, the Breton-born Budoc apparently spent some years as a child with his mother in exile in Cornwall, before returning to his native country where he became a monk. In the year 500, at the age of eighty-three, he died at Dol and was buried there. A ninth-century life of Winwaloe (3 March) mentions that he lived on the island of Laurea and, judging by dedications to him in Cornwall, Devon and Wales, he must at some time have returned for a while to Britain.

The legend of his birth bears a strong resemblance to that of several other Celtic saints, such as Kentigern (13 January) and Cenydd (27 June). In this story, Budoc's father, egged on by his jealous mother-in-law, who declared that the forthcoming baby was not his, put his wife in a barrel and cast her into the sea. As the wretched woman tossed about on the waves, the spirit of Brigid (1 February) who looks after women in labour, comforted her as she gave birth to her son. Mother and infant were then floated ashore on the Irish coast, the mother becoming a washerwoman in a monastery near Waterford, where her son was educated.

FINNIAN OF CLONARD 12 December

Traditionally the teacher of the Twelve Apostles of Ireland, several of whom lived before his time, Finnian was born in Leinster towards the end of the fifth century. As a young man he crossed the water to study monasticism in Wales, and on his return to Ireland established at least two monasteries of his own before finally settling his most important foundation at Clonard in County Meath, a place with which his name is eternally linked.

A life of this saint, written in the tenth century, claims that at least three thousand monks came to Clonard to follow his teaching. Many of them were later sent on their way, bearing a crozier and a gospel book, to establish their own settlements. At Clonard, Finnian offered a rigorous study of the scriptures and of the writings of the early Fathers, as well as practical experience of the type of monasticism he had found in Wales, mingled with his understanding of the desert communities of the early Coptic church.

His penitentiary, partly based on the work of Jerome and

Cassian, is the earliest of its kind. It proved to be a major
influence on the one drawn up by Columbanus (21 November).
In the middle of the sixth century an attack of the yellow plague
swept over Ireland, and in 549 Finnian contracted it at Clonard and
died. We do not know the exact circumstances of his death, but
somehow he appears to have put himself at risk in order that his
monks might be spared the infection: we are told that he died
to save the 'people of the Gael' from perishing of the pestilence.

Thou God of Life

Bless, O God, the thing on which mine eye doth rest,
Bless, O God, the thing on which my hope doth rest,
Bless, O God, my reason and my purpose,
Bless, O bless Thou them, Thou God of life;
> Bless, O God, my reason and my purpose,
> Bless, O bless Thou them, Thou God of life.

Collected by Alexander Carmichael

FINGAR AND PIALA 14 December

Sometime in the middle of the fifth century, Fingar and Piala,
brother and sister, were killed at Hayle in Cornwall on the orders of
the pagan king of the tribe of Dumnonia. They had been converted
to Christianity by Patrick (17 March) and driven out of their native
Ireland by their royal father, infuriated that they had taken on the
new religion. They went first to Brittany, where Fingar's feast is
still kept, before making their final voyage to Cornwall.

Chief of Chiefs

God with me lying down,
God with me rising up,
God with me in each ray of light,
Nor I a ray of joy without Him,
> Nor one ray without Him.

Christ with me sleeping,
Christ with me waking,
Christ with me watching,
Every day and night,
    Each day and night.

God with me protecting,
The Lord with me directing,
The Spirit with me strengthening,
For ever and for evermore,
    Ever and evermore, Amen.
        Chief of chiefs, Amen.

Collected by Alexander Carmichael

SAMTHANN   18 December

With a herd of only six cows, to emphasize the poverty of the convent that she established at Clonroney, County Longford, Samthann, who died in 739, inspired many of the leaders of the reform movement known as the *Céli Dé* (the servants of God) by the simplicity of her life. Her disciples included Maelruan (7 July).

Samthann is mentioned in both the canon and the litany of the *Stowe Missal* (a late eighth-century compilation, now in the library of the Royal Irish Academy in Dublin), and her cult spread to the Continent through the teachings of Virgil (27 November). Several of her sayings have been preserved for us. Two concerning pilgrimages have her advising a disciple to remember that 'The distance to heaven is the same from every end of the earth and if a person comes close to God he cannot be far from home' and emphasizing that 'The kingdom of heaven can be reached from every land'. And when the same disciple also told her that he was going to give up study and concentrate solely on prayer, she asked him 'What then can give your mind stability that it wander not, if you neglect spiritual study?'

Pictish Stone, Aberlemno

FLANNAN   18 December

A disciple of Molua (4 August), Flannan succeeded him as Abbot of
Killaloe, where he is said to have established the stone oratory that
stands by the cathedral. As a wandering preacher, who possibly
visited the Isle of Man, Flannan is also honoured in Scotland.
The outlying Flannan Islands to the west of Lewis bear his
name, and the monastic ruins on one of them, known as the
chapel of Flannan, were regarded as a sacred place at least until
the seventeenth century.

My God and my Chief

My God and my Chief,
   I seek to Thee in the morning,
My God and my Chief,
   I seek to Thee this night.
I am giving Thee my mind,
   I am giving Thee my will,
I am giving Thee my wish,
   My soul everlasting and my body.

Mayest Thou be chieftain over me,
Mayest Thou be master unto me,
Mayest Thou be shepherd over me,
Mayest Thou be guardian unto me,
Mayest Thou be herdsman over me,
Mayest Thou be guide unto me,
Mayest Thou be with me, O Chief of chiefs,
Father everlasting and God of the heavens.

Collected by Alexander Carmichael

TATHAN/TATHEUS 26 December

The son of an Irish prince, Tathan came to Wales in the late fifth century and established his monastic college at Caerwent, a few miles to the west of Chepstow. There, Cadoc (25 September) became one of his disciples.

There are two conflicting theories as to how Tathan made the journey from Ireland to Wales. One account suggests that he sailed up the Bristol Channel into the mouth of the Severn, possibly making a landing at Portskewett on the west bank, rather than travelling up the Wye to Chepstow. Professor E. G. Bowen, however, thought it more possible that the saint landed in North Wales and journeyed overland to the south-east.

Legend favours the first alternative. For it tells us that Tathan came to Gwent by boat; and that when he landed a stag stood on the mooring rope to keep it fast while the saint evangelized the area. Moreover when Tathan and his companions returned to their craft, the stag knelt down and offered its body as food for the company. A. R. Utting in a booklet about the myths connected with Tewdric (1 April) suggests that this stag represents the cloven-footed, horned God Cernunnos, who like the Greek Pan was a fertility figure and given the image of the devil by the Christians. As such he symbolizes Tathan's encounter with pagan tribes.

We are on surer ground if we actually go inland to the still-walled town of Roman Caerwent, where the legions were stationed and where the powerful Celtic tribe of the Silures had their seat of government and main trading place. Here excavations have revealed a Romano-Celtic sixth-century church, whose basilica structure suggests a link with a similar building in the Roman

Tathan

town of Silchester in the Thames Valley. This led Professor E. G. Bowen to believe that it was built by people fleeing west from the Saxon invaders and carrying their style of architecture with them.

Dr V.E. Nash Williams, however, in his study of early Christian monuments in Wales, thinks that this building could actually be of Byzantine origin, and that its construction was influenced by merchants from the East using the western seaways.

Either way, it is most probable that the church was built on the site of Tathan's monastery, fairly soon after his death. Certainly he was much beloved in the old Roman city, that remained a focal point of trade routes long after the legions departed. Tathan was to leave behind him a reputation as a miracle worker, but beyond that he was known with affection as the father of all the woodlands of the county of Gwent, and remembered as a wise, hospitable man, who never gave way to anger.

Place I in Thee my hope, O God,
My living hope in the Father of the heavens,
My great hope to be with Thyself
    In the distant world to come.

Father and Son and Spirit,
    The One Person of the Three,
Perfect, world without end,
    Changeless through life eternal.

    Collected by Alexander Carmichael

DECEMBER PILGRIMAGE

Flannan's Shrine, Killaloe

If you are fortunate enough to be able to reserve a visit to New Grange for the winter solstice (only a few people can be taken into the cairn each year), first make a pilgrimage to the west. If you follow the River Shannon north-east to Killaloe on the southern tip of Lough Derg, you will find the cathedral where Flannan's relics were enshrined, beneath the steep slopes of Slieve Bernagh. The medieval building still contains stones with ogham and runic inscriptions, and the more ancient structure in the churchyard is said to have been Flannan's oratory. Another saint is associated with this town who is Flannan's predecessor, Molua, of whom virtually nothing is known, although a feast for him was kept on 4 August. His oratory stands beside the Catholic church, having been removed from Friar's Island in the Lough, when the Shannon hydro-electric scheme of 1929 put it in danger.

To the West of Killaloe are the standing stones of the prehistoric ritual site at Craggaunowen.

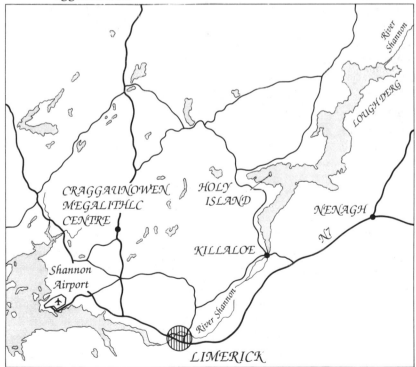

January

Celtic Art

In 1891, a second-century BC vessel was found in a Danish bog. Careful cleaning revealed a gilded silver cauldron, covered both within and without by exuberant and sophisticated engravings, in which the representation of natural figures and animals jostled with symbolic creatures to create a world of myths and history. Together, the craftsmanship and content of the design give us a lively idea of the Celtic art that flourished throughout central Europe and along the Atlantic seaboard before the Christian era. It was a tradition that was to be enhanced as the Celts, who had always used pictorial art and symbols to express their intimations of the supernatural world, were further enriched by the coming of Christianity.

With the spread of the Roman empire much of the pre-Christian Celtic art on the Continent ceased to flourish; only in Ireland, where the legions never set foot, did it persist. So that, when Christian symbolism became current there, it was grafted on to an art form that was already rich in esoteric meaning. We see it expressed in the carvings on the high stone crosses set up wherever a monastic settlement was founded, in many of the croziers and bell shrines that have been preserved, and above all in the engravings of the Ardagh chalice in the National Museum in Dublin.

For most of us, however, the experience of Celtic art is most easily available through many excellent reproductions of the illustrated manuscripts designed and executed by monastic scribes. Here the texts are inter-leaved with the so-called carpet pages, covered in intricate designs whose resemblance to Islamic patterning is only part of the story: the Celts had no inhibitions about representing the human form, and in their geometric constructions there is a purposeful design that goes beyond aesthetic delight. As Hilary Richardson writes in the essay on

Celtic art in James P. Mackey's *Introduction to Celtic Christianity* (*see* Bibliography), 'the eye is led on without rest' for these designs are 'not so much religious art as liturgical . . . constructed to aid contemplation and prayer'. In studying these pages, we do well to take note of the advice given by the twelfth-century Gerald of Wales who in his travels through Ireland found nothing among the many marvels at Brigid's Kildare more miraculous than a 'wonderful book which they say was written at the dictation of an angel during the lifetime of the virgin'. He goes on to warn his readers to look most carefully at such manuscripts, for:

> If you look at them carelessly and casually and not too closely, you may judge them to be mere daubs rather than careful compositions. You will see nothing subtle where everything is subtle. But if you take the trouble to look very closely, and penetrate with your eyes to the secret of the artistry, you will notice such intricacies, so delicate and subtle, so close together and well-knitted, so involved and bound together, and so fresh still in their colourings that you will not hesitate to declare that all these things must have been the result of the work, not of men, but of angels.

When we turn from the physical aspect of these manuscripts to their content, that is as we move from visual art to literature, we find the same rich inventiveness and exuberance. Of course much of the work was a matter of dedicated calligraphy, the copying of gospel texts as authorized by St Jerome; but even then many of the scribes could not resist adding a few marginal notes.

Such scribbling was no doubt thought of as ephemeral, but there is also a body of religious and secular literature that shows how the Celtic love of oral poetry and story-telling was beginning to take a written form through the quills and brushes of the monastic scribes of the seventh and eighth centuries.

The oldest surviving Eucharistic hymn in Europe was written in Latin in the antiphonary compiled at the monastic college of Bangor in Northern Ireland between 680 and 691; which also contains a hymn in honour of the martyrs. As for secular poetry, we have the nature lyrics of Columcille of Iona, homesick for the oak groves of Derry; and a wealth of tales from Irish history and folklore, written down by monastic scribes in the early eighth century.

I have wondered how much of this work was undertaken in the short, cold days of January, when it is impossible to cultivate the land or go about such outdoor occupations as made up the work of the monastery. The answer comes in part in a letter, which Sister Benedicta Ward quotes in *The Venerable Bede* (Geoffrey Chapman, 1990). Writing to a continental bishop, an abbot of Jarrow apologizes for not sending more copies of Bede's verse and prose lives of Cuthbert because 'The conditions of the past winter oppressed the island of our race very horribly with cold and ice and long and widespread storms of wind and rain, so that the hand of the scribe was hindered from producing a great number of books'.

Blessing of the Kindling

I will kindle my fire this morning
In presence of the holy angels of heaven,
In presence of Ariel of the loveliest form,
In presence of Uriel of the myriad charms,
Without malice, without jealousy, without envy,
Without fear, without terror of any one under the sun,
But the Holy Son of God to shield me.
    Without malice, without jealousy, without envy,
    Without fear, without terror of any one under the sun,
    But the Holy Son of God to shield me.

Collected by Alexander Carmichael

The Guiding Light of Eternity

O God, who broughtest me from the rest of last night
Upon the joyous light of this day,
Be Thou bringing me from the new light of this day
Unto the guiding light of eternity.
    Oh! from the new light of this day
    Unto the guiding light of eternity.

Collected by Alexander Carmichael

MOLLIEN   6 January

An obscure saint, possibly from Brittany, who was the original
patron of Mullion on the west coast of the Lizard Peninsula in
Cornwall.

BRANNOC   7 January

The wide fields, still laid out according to a Saxon plan, that cover
Braunton Burrows in north Devon, were said to have been first
cultivated by Brannoc, a wandering saint of uncertain date who,
according to the sixteenth-century John Leland, lies buried beneath
the high altar of Braunton parish church.

    The legend is that Brannoc came to Devon from Brittany,
sailing round Land's End in a stone coffin, which is probably a
good way to describe the frail craft, ballasted with stone, which
undertook that journey. Many such boats must have been wrecked
on the Cornish rocks. Brannoc, however, came safely ashore and

Braunton Piglets

responded to the vision that bade him establish a church at the place where he found a white sow with a litter of piglets. In the Middle Ages, the people of Braunton celebrated their founder by carving pigs on the roof bosses and bench ends of the new church built over Brannoc's tomb.

Pigs had a particular significance for the Celts, who associated them with the Other World, a belief which is clearly shown in the Arthurian legends of huge boar hunts. We also find that in Irish and Welsh traditions, swineherds, despite their servile occupation, have great gifts of prophecy, giving them a curious status in courtly society. In short, pigs, and particularly sows, were thought to be possessed of wisdom that humankind did well to heed. Brannoc was not the only saint to let pigs indicate where a settlement was to be made.

NATHALAN 8 January

Born of a noble family at the beginning of the seventh century on the east coast of Scotland, Nathalan decided to show his devotion to God by spending his life cultivating the earth. As a result, he grew vegetables enough to feed people in times of famine.

FILLAN 9 January

A nephew of Comgan (13 October), Fillan lived in the first half of the eighth century. He was born in Ireland but came to Scotland as a boy with his widowed mother who had resolved to end her days in the convent on the island of Inchcailloch in the southern waters of Loch Lomond. He was to spend the rest of his life among the Scots, dwelling as a hermit at Pittenweem in Fife and then becoming a wandering priest in Perthshire. Finally, he established a monastery to the south of Tyndrum on the banks of the River Dochart that flows into Loch Tay, a place that walkers will reach along the West Highland Way.

An early medieval priory, which flourished until the twelfth century, stood on the site of Fillan's monastery, and near its ruins there is a pool whose waters, endowed with the power of the saint, were said to cure madness. The cure, was a harsh one, for the mad person had to be immersed in the waters and then spend the following night bound to a wooden frame in the priory church, his head lying in the stone font, which you will still find there.

Fillan's cult was to become so important throughout Scotland, that Robert the Bruce carried the reliquary containing his arm bone to the battle of Bannockburn. It was said that when Fillan was alive, a light shone out of this arm, enabling him to write in the dark. The handbell that he used to summon his flock to prayer is now in the National Museum of Antiquities in Edinburgh.

DERMOT   10 January

In the sixth century, Dermot, a colleague of Senan (8 March), founded a monastery on the island of Innis Clothran in Lough Ree, Ireland. Ruins of six churches still survive there, and the island has long been a place of pilgrimage.

The Three

> In name of Father,
> In name of Son,
> In name of Spirit,
>   Three in One:
>
> Father cherish me,
> Son cherish me,
> Spirit cherish me,
>   Three all-kindly.

Collected by Alexander Carmichael

KENTIGERN   13 January

Kentigern, the founder of Glasgow, grandson of King Loth, was born in the latter half of the sixth century. The legends surrounding his birth, that have come down to us from the Middle Ages, make him into one of those heroes of folklore whose mothers are cast out to give birth in circumstances of incredible hardship. In this case, Kentigern's mother, Loth's daughter Thaneukes (a name that became transmuted to Enoch, and is remembered in Glasgow's Enoch Square), longed to give birth without knowing a man.

As a punishment for presuming to imitate the Blessed Virgin, she was raped; and having incurred the wrath of her father by her subsequent pregnancy, she was put in a wagon and pushed backwards over the cliffs of her father's royal palace. You can still see the place where this drop is said to have taken place from the summit of the hill fort on Traprain Law, an outcrop of volcanic rock jutting out of the rich Lothian farmlands to the east of Edinburgh. Miraculously the wagon righted itself when it reached the ground and Thaneukes was unscathed, but Loth's wrath was unappeased and he cast his daughter out in a coracle into the waters of the Firth of Forth. All the fish in the Forth escorted her boat safely to the Isle of May, from whence she went north to land safely at Culross. There she lit a fire by the shore and her baby was born.

Some shepherds hearing the cries of the mother and child ran to tell the holy hermit Serf (1 July) who dwelt nearby what they had found. To their surprise he was already aware that a marvellous and significant birth had taken place for he had just heard a heavenly choir singing the Gloria. He welcomed the child, calling him Mungo, which means my dear one, as well as giving him the formal name of Kentigern, the Capital Lord.

Jocelyn, a twelfth-century monk of Furness, who wrote a life of Kentigern, tells of the many miracles wrought by him while he was being educated at Culross, before, as a young man, he set out on his own mission. The story of his link with Glasgow came about through his friendship with Fergus, an old man whom he met soon after leaving Serf. When Fergus came to die, he was put into a cart drawn by untamed bulls. Once these animals reached the Clyde, they refused to move further, stopping at a place which had been hallowed by Ninian (26 August), which has since become Glasgow. There Fergus was buried, and Kentigern hung his hand-bell on the branch of a tree to call the people to prayer. This story was partly told to explain why, at such a very young age, Kentigern should have been consecrated as Bishop of Strathclyde.

His wanderings were not over however, for he travelled on missionary journeys to the north-east, before being compelled for political reasons to flee the country and journey south through Cumbria into North Wales. There he is said to have befriended Asaph (1 May) and helped him to establish the settlement in Clwyd that still bears his name.

In 573, Rhydderch Heal, the King of Strathclyde, commanded Kentigern to return to his native land, for the pagan forces that

Kentigern

threatened him had been defeated. So the Bishop journeyed north through Cumbria to meet the King at Hoddum near the River Annan, on ground that rose to enable the crowds of people who had come to witness the event to have a fine view of the encounter. (The same story of the earth rising is told about the synod at Llanddewi Brefi when David (1 March) attacked the Pelagian heresy.)

Some time after his return to Glasgow, Kentigern is said to have met Columcille (9 June). The two man exchanged pastoral staffs, and the one that Columcille gave to Kentigern was inlaid with gold. It was reported to have been kept in Ripon Cathedral until the fifteenth century.

Kentigern died on the Feast of Epiphany in 612, comforted, so his biographers tell us, by the glory of the Lord, and conversing to the last with his guardian angels. He is said to have reached the astonishing age of 181.

ITA   15 January

The two leading woman saints of Ireland are Brigid (1 February) and Ita, who lived some fifty years later, dying around 570. Ita established her convent near Limerick. Many of the saints of Ireland came there to be taught by her, and she is supposed to have given Brendan (16 May) a triad of doctrines, telling him that God loved three things: a pure heart, a simple life and a generous charity.

Ita is mentioned in Alcuin's poem on the Irish saints and described as 'the foster mother of all the saints of Ireland'. She is said to have composed a lullaby for the infant Jesus, and to have prayed that God's son from heaven might be given to her in the form of a baby that she could nurse. In a vision, that prayer was granted and she came to share with Brigid the role of Christ's wet nurse.

FURSEY   16 January

Bede (27 May) tells us that Fursey, born on the shores of Lough Corrib, Galway, at the end of the sixth century, was 'of noble Irish blood and even more noble in mind than in birth; for from his boyhood he had not only read sacred books and observed monastic discipline but, as is fitting in saints, had also diligently practised all that he learned'. He was determined from an early age 'to spend his life as a pilgrim for love of our Lord'. Accordingly, about 630, accompanied by Foillan (30 October), he journeyed across Britain to the province of the East Angles and set up his monastery by the deserted Roman fort of Burgh Castle. After a while he fell ill and during his nights of delirium he was granted a series of visions. One of them recorded by Bede is of poignant relevance to our own time and the burning of the Kuwaiti oil wells in the early 1990s, for Fursey looking down on the earth from a great height saw a gloomy valley where four fires burnt. When he asked his angel guides what these flames meant, he was told that in time they would consume the whole world. The fires he saw were called Falsehood, Covetousness, Discord and Cruelty.

When Sigebert, King of East Anglia, was killed in battle against the King of Mercia, Fursey sailed to Gaul and was given land to establish a monastery at Lagny on the River Marne to the east of Paris. His cult was to flourish throughout Picardy and when he died, at Mézerolles in 650, his relics were translated to Péronne, a monastery which was ruled according to the teachings of Patrick (17 March) and which possessed early copies of Patrick's confessional and epistle. It was to become a hostel for pilgrims journeying to Rome and the Holy Land.

DAY 18 January

Patron of the mining village of this name near Redruth in Cornwall, Day (or Dei) is probably the same as a Breton Abbot of Landevennec who lived on the coast near Brest.

BRANWALADER 19 January

In the Exeter martyrology, Branwalader is described as the son of the Cornish king, Kenan. He seems to have been of Welsh origin, however, and to have travelled with Samson (28 July) to the Channel Islands and Brittany. His cult was flourishing in the tenth century when Athelstan obtained his relics and brought them back to Britain, giving them into the keeping of the monastery of Milton in Dorset.

FECHIN   20 January

In the middle of the seventh century, Fechin, who came from Forre
in West Meath, established his monastery off the High Island (Ard
Oilen) which is joined at low tide to the coast of Connemara. There
the ruins of the beehive cells that housed his monks can still be seen.
As at Skellig Michael, where another Celtic monastery survives,
there is no beach to Fechin's island and to reach its summit you
must climb up steep cliffs. On the mainland a well dedicated to
this saint can be found on the northern pass over the Mamturk
Mountains.

God's Aid

God to enfold me,
    God to surround me,
God in my speaking,
    God in my thinking.

God in my sleeping,
    God in my waking,
God in my watching,
    God in my hoping.

God in my life,
    God in my lips,
God in my soul,
    God in my heart.

Collected by Alexander Carmichael

Prayer

Thanks to Thee ever, O gentle Christ,
    That Thou hast raised me freely from the black
And from the darkness of last night
    To the kindly light of this day.

Praise unto Thee, O God of all creatures,
    According to each life Thou hast poured on me,
My desire, my word, my sense, my repute,
    My thought, my deed, my way, my fame.

Collected by Alexander Carmichael

Prayer for the Day

Pray I this day my prayer to Thee, O God,
Voice I this day as voices the voice of Thy mouth,
Keep I this day as keep the people of heaven,
Spend I this day as spend Thine own household,

Go I this day according to Thy laws, O God,
Pass I this day as pass the saints in heaven.

Each thing I have received from Thee it came,
Each thing for which I hope, from Thy love it will come,
Each thing I enjoy, it is of Thy bounty,
Each thing I ask, comes of Thy disposing.

Collected by Alexander Carmichael

GILDAS 29 January

Much of our knowledge of the sixth-century world in which the
Celtic church flourished comes from the writings of the monk
Gildas. A northerner, he was born in 498 within the shadow of
Hadrian's Wall, which he accurately described as a fairly useless
construction, 'being made of turf rather than stone: so it did no
good'. Later he went to the monastic college founded by St Illtyd
(6 November), whom he described as 'the refined master of all
Britain'.

He was forty-three when he started to write his main work, *The
Ruin of Britain*, a diatribe against the corruption of the church of
his day and its falling away from the purity of its early intentions.
According to his biographer Caradoc of Llancarfan, much of his
writing was done on an island in the Bristol Channel but he does
not seem able to decide whether this hermitage was on Somerset's
Steep Holm or the Welsh Flat Holm. Current folklore, which the
cynics attribute to the Victorian romantics, makes Steep Holm the
favourite candidate, for it is here that visitors claim to have heard
the monk's measured ghostly footsteps around the scant ruins
of the medieval priory. Gildas had another, mainland, hermitage
at Street, where the road to Somerton runs now: and he was
obviously closely connected with the monastery at Glastonbury
4 miles (6 km) away.

After a visit to Ireland at the age of sixty-seven, he is said to have settled in southern Brittany near the place in Morbihan that bears his name. It is probable that it was during this period of his life that he wrote many letters, of which a few fragments fortunately remain. As we come up to the six weeks of Lent, it is good to remember his wise words on fasting, contained in one such fragment:

> Abstinence from bodily food is useless without charity. Those who do not fast unduly or abstain overmuch from God's creation, while being careful in the sight of God to preserve within them a clean heart (on which, as they know, their life ultimately depends), are better than those who do not eat flesh or take pleasure in the food of this world, or travel in carriages or on horseback, and so regard themselves as superior to the rest of men: to these death has entered through the windows of their pride.

(Gildas, of course, wrote in Latin. I have used the translation of his writing which Michael Winterbottom prepared for his book on Gildas in Phillimore's series *History from the Sources*.)

The *Welsh Annals* record that Gildas died in 570.

MAEDOC OF FERNS   31 January

An Irishman, born in the latter part of the sixth century, Maedoc was educated in the austere regime established by David (1 March) in Pembrokeshire. When he returned to Ireland to found his own monasteries at Drumlane and Rossinver, he is said to have continued living with extreme frugality and discipline, reciting five hundred psalms daily and living for seven years on barley bread and water. He died in 626. His crozier can be seen in the National Museum in Dublin and his handbell and reliquary are in the library of Armagh Cathedral.

JANUARY PILGRIMAGE

Fillan's Chapel by Tyndrum, Strath Fillan

It is a challenge to walk in the Highlands in January, but this pilgrimage only involves a short part of the West Highland Way between Tyndrum and Glen Dochart, and it is good to be there when the nearby road is free of traffic. After leaving Tyndrum, you will come, after a mile or so (1½ km), to the place where Fillan established his monastery early in the eighth century. The ruins of a medieval priory mark the spot now; they stand beside the old road, which runs through the farmstead and agricultural research station of Kirkton.

Follow the West Highland Way a little further until you reach the farm of Auchter Fyre. As you come to the farm, you will find that the farm road takes you over a stream cascading gently into the Dochart. Once

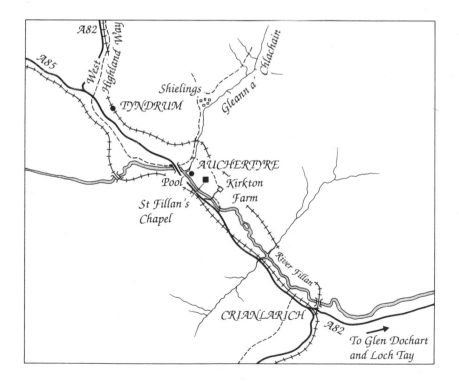

across the bridge the road veers west to follow the course of the stream towards the river. Just beyond the confluence, there is the pool, whose waters, blessed by Fillan, were believed to cure madness. Well into the nineteenth century they were used for that purpose.

Imbolc

The coming of the Light
The Time of the Lactation of the Ewes

 # Mark

This evangelist, whose symbol is a lion, and whose feast falls on 25 April, is the appropriate gospel writer for Imbolc, a time of roaring storms. The racy style of his writing is appropriate too. Mark is breathless to bring us the good news, rushing 'straightway' from one event in the life of Christ to the next, and telling his story as though it had all happened yesterday or even an hour ago. Yet, although his gospel was written about 70 CE, and so nearer in time to the events he describes than those of the other three evangelists, most early Christian writers tended to ignore him, for they found little in his work that is not contained in the more elaborate versions of Matthew and Luke.

I have yet to find references to Mark in the lives of the Celtic saints, who mostly turned to John. Yet he is, of course, always included in the gospel books; and those learned men were no doubt aware of the tradition that Mark's gospel was dictated by Peter, and of the pronouncement in 130 by Papias, Bishop of Hierapolis, that 'Mark, having become the interpreter of Peter, wrote down accurately all that he remembered of the things done and said by the Lord'. This, as the actor Alec McCowen remarked in his *Personal Mark* (Hamish Hamilton, 1984), results in the picture of Jesus as a real person, not 'a solemn, bearded schoolmaster'. In presenting, as the agnostic McCowen sees it, 'an ordinary man with extraordinary powers', Mark brings home to us the stance of the Celtic saints and mystics who never denied their common humanity or lost touch with the people they lived amongst.

 # February

Mary of the Gael

At the start of this month, we pay tribute to Brigid, and at Candlemas on the second day celebrate the purification of the Virgin Mary. It is a solemn and joyful time: the ending of the darkness as the seed of light which was planted at the solstice in the womb-like depths of such carefully constructed passage graves as New Grange (see p. 46), gradually pushes its way into the air. The weather in these islands may often be more cold and threatening now than ever it was at mid-winter, so that the survival of the new-born lambs is a great marvel, but even if there is not much warmth in the sun, the hours of daylight increase.

A Jungian psychologist, Wendy Robinson, has described the *animus* (the unconscious male element in women, corresponding to the *anima* in the unconscious of a man) as having the form of a knife or of light. As we meditate on the role of women in the Celtic church, we will discover that both these aspects are apparent, as they are in the feminist movement today.

I will look first at the knife, the implement that signifies gender equality, a phallic tool for cutting away punishing social, educational and economic distinctions. The Celts were largely free of such inequalities: girls were taught alongside their brothers at the colleges and schools attached to monastic institutions such as Clonard in Ireland, Ninian's Candida Casa in Scotland, and Illtyd's foundation on the coast of Glamorgan. Above all, like the Israeli girls today, they were expected to fight alongside the men, an important matter in a society continually torn by tribal battles and disputes. High-born women in particular would be expected to exercise the sort of leadership shown by such a warrior queen as Boudicca of the Iceni. Although their words have not come down to us, I am sure that the bards extolled her courage through many generations. She would have been an example to the Celtic women of the fifth century, who had to take their part in quelling the Saxon invaders. It was not until the seventh century that Adomnan, a Donegal-born Abbot of Iona, formulated his rule which finally exempted women from military service.

When the knife had played its part, it could be transformed into a flame of light that would start to dispel chaos and the darkness of warfare and its attendant plagues. In their worship of the goddess, the early Celts knew this, in common with all primitive peoples, so in story after story the world over we find the goddess earth-linked as Demeter was; and in the Irish creation myths, the primordial Cessair and Banba are associated respectively with the flood waters and the land that emerges from the waters. Women are the very matter of creation and, in the Christian era, we find Mary, as the Queen-Maiden of the sea as well as the Queen-Maiden of the earth, being addressed in the songs collected by Alexander Carmichael throughout the Highlands and Islands in the nineteenth century as 'the corn of the land' and 'the treasury of the sea'.

The nurturing aspect of the life of each individual woman is a natural corollary of this deep-held faith in the link between the feminine and the essential rhythms of nature. Over and over again in the songs which the women sang as they went about the daily tasks of lighting a fire in the morning, leaving it to smoulder in the evening, preparing meals, weaving cloth, caring for children and milking the cows, the female guardians of earth and water are invoked. Here are two verses of a butter-making song, drawn from Alexander Carmichael's collection and quoted by Esther de Waal in *A World Made Whole* (Fount, 1991):

> Come, thou Brigit, handmaid calm;
> Hasten the butter on the cream;
> Seest thou impatient Peter yonder
> Waiting the buttered bannock white and yellow.
>
> Come, thou Mary Mother mild,
> Hasten the butter on the cream;
> Seest thou Paul and John and Jesus
> Waiting the gracious butter yonder.

She also quotes verses from a song used in 'waulking' cloth, that is stretching the woven material on a frame to strengthen and thicken it. As she prepares her cloth, the woman thinks of her family:

> This is not cloth for priest or cleric
> But it is cloth for my own little Donald of love,
> For my companion beloved, for John of joy,
> And for Muriel of loveliest hue.

She also sings for herself and her sisters as they go about this task, asking God that He will:

> Place Thou thine arm around
> Each woman who shall be waulking it,
> And do Thou aid her in the hour
> Of her need.

These two verses emphasize the dual aspect of woman's nature. She is concerned with the solid and earthy, and in moulding the tangible to the needs of her family; at the same time she is always close to the unearthly and the otherworld of spirit. Perhaps it is in an attempt to embrace this dichotomy that the mothers of so many of the Celtic saints (including the mother of Brigid) are not spoken of as married matrons, but as victims of rape or at best as being involved with an illicit love, an absence of spouse which echoes Mary's own conception and pregnancy. Brigid's mother, Broiccseach, was a maidservant, seduced by her master Dubtach, prince of Leinster, whose wife was so jealous that she had the girl and her child sold into slavery. So the child Brigid had no earthly home, and it is even said that she was born on a threshold neither within nor without a house.

Similarly, Non, the mother of David of Wales, was seduced by the king of Ceredigion, and when the time came for her to be delivered, her child was born in a great storm on the cliffs above St Bride's Bay, where two stones appeared out of the earth so that her labour would be commemorated for ever.

I believe that such stories are hinting at some truth behind the mysteries of birth and nurture, the fruits of the land and the seductive threat of the sea. In our own time many people see this truth in terms of Gaia and the goddess; or, in the words of Julian of Norwich, as the 'Motherhood of God'. Those of us who feel God to be more a verb than a noun, a constant act of creation and harmonizing, are happier perhaps with the Jewish concept of the Shekinnah, the awareness of the presence of God, in feminine form. It is from that stance that I approach Brigid herself, and the other saints of the new, cold light of February. Brigid's flower is the delicate snowdrop which it is said should never be brought inside a house.

Brigid

BRIGID   1 February

It is hard to separate the historical Brigid, who died in the first quarter of the sixth century, and whose feast we celebrate today, from the spiritual Brigid, who has affinity with the mother of the Celtic gods and with the Virgin Mary. The problem is accentuated by the fact that her festival falls on the day of Imbolc, the Celtic season that marks the coming of the light after the dark days of winter, and that tomorrow we shall celebrate Our Lady's feast of Candlemas.

The historical Brigid was the Abbess of Kildare in the central plain of Ireland, a place whose name indicates that she had her church in an oak grove, a place that was undoubtedly once sacred to the Druids. Here, by the walls of her abbey, a fire was tended by her nuns, and only women were allowed near it. This fire is said to have been kept perpetually alight for nearly a thousand years after her death.

The monastery at Kildare contained both men and women, and in managing it, Brigid must have shown the organizing ability, energy and commonsense of Theresa of Avila, who also combined worldly wisdom with spiritual insights. It is this venture into the spiritual, timeless world that makes nonsense of chronology and enabled the tradition that makes Brigid a contemporary of Mary. One account would have her as the daughter of the inn keeper who turned the Holy Family from his door; and all versions equate her with Maia of the Byzantine tradition, who acted both as midwife and wet nurse to the infant Jesus. In the songs which Alexander Carmichael collected throughout the Hebrides, she is referred to as 'the aid-woman of the Mother of Nazarus' and she performs similar services for the 'mothers of Uist in their humble homes'. The women who passed this tradition on to their daughters, and who called on Brigid when their time came, had the sense of a spirit transcending the historical nun, however good and holy her life had been. With the Druids' firm belief in reincarnation still running in their veins, they may well have felt that the inn keeper's daughter had returned to fifth-century Ireland as Brigid, the baptized daughter of a pagan prince, born out of wedlock and brought up by Druids.

Their beliefs could go even deeper than that. As we may understand Mary as the willing means by which the Spirit came to be realized on earth, so Brigid is the all-provider, the nurturer, enabling the Spirit to survive in bodily form. For this reason she is thought of as wet nurse as well as midwife, a belief that extended to the legend that she owned a cow which would give milk sufficient for her needs at any time. Furthermore, the golden-haired Brigid was invoked for the care of the crofters' cattle.

She is also the patron of poets, smiths and healers, and in these three aspects of her care we meet the tripartite goddess: the young girl, the muse of the poets; the matron, whose skill, like that of the smith's, lies in shaping the material world; and the crone, the old woman, whose wisdom enables her to heal. In all three aspects she is grounded in the common humanity of all women. It is well that we celebrate her in this cruel winter month, when the lambs are born, and the ewes' milk, at a time when most of the cows would be dry, could supplement the scarce diet of Samhain.

SERIOL 1 February

At the south-eastern tip of Anglesey, off-shore from the site of the Augustinian priory ruins of Penmon, lies the virtually

Penmon Priory

inaccessible island of Priestholm also known as Puffin Island. Geraldus Cambrensis, writing towards the end of the twelfth century, said that it was 'inhabited by hermits, living by manual labour and serving God'. 'It is remarkable' he continued, 'that when, by the influence of human passions, any discord arises among them, all their provisions are devoured and infected by a species of small mice, with which the island abounds; but when the discord ceases they are no longer infected.'

Those hermits were probably descendants of the monks of the sixth century who settled here under the guidance of Seriol, who had his own hermitage by his well on the mainland. The enclosure in which he dwelt lies to the seaward side of the abbey church, and still retains the peace that was so obviously an essential element of his community.

The Dream of the Virgin

Lady Mary the fair in her bed lay sleeping
When a dream to her came;
Her Son was passing and passing before her,
And gazed straight in her face.

Breton ballad

IA (IVE)   3 February

The daughter of a Munster chieftain, Ia came to Cornwall with a group of Irish missionaries led by Gwinear (23 March). The tradition which has it that she sailed across the sea on an enormous leaf probably refers to the long, leaf-shaped Irish curragh, in which she undoubtedly made the journey. Dinan, a powerful local chieftain, became her patron and at her request built a church on the north Cornish coast, at the place now known as St Ives. From there she went to her martyrdom in Brittany, taking with her, it is said, 777 disciples.

TRESAN 7 February

With six brothers and three sisters, the sixth-century Tresan left his native Ireland to settle at Mareuil on the River Marne in France. There he lived as a swineherd, every day driving the pigs to the door of the ancient church of St Martin so that he could listen to Mass. His piety was observed and in the course of time he was ordained priest and officiated at this same church. The story goes that once when he was particularly weary after a long journey, he thrust his staff into the ground on his return to Mareuil, and lay down to sleep. When he awoke the staff had taken root and budded into leaf.

KEW 8 February

With her brother Docco, Kew sailed from Gwent in South Wales and landed in Cornwall near Wadebridge, where a village, originally called Lan Docco, still bears her name; and where until the fifteenth century a chapel dedicated to her stood by the church. There is a story that Docco would not allow his sister near his hermit's cell until he saw her take command of a wild boar. This reminds us of the particular significance that pigs had for the Celts, as creatures connected with the other world; so when Docco realized that his sister must have supernatural powers he talked with her and found her to be full of rare virtue and holiness.

We do not know the dates of Docco and Kew, but they probably belonged to the late fifth century, for they were no longer in Cornwall in the first part of the sixth century when Samson (28 July) embarked on his missionary journeys, and made Lan Docco his first place to visit. There we are told he was greeted not by the founders of the settlement but by one Junavius (whose Latin name is derived from the Cornish word for light) who entertained him with great hospitality.

TEILO   9 February

Born in Pembrokeshire, some time in the sixth century, Teilo spent almost his entire working life in the moorland hills and steep valleys of Llandeilo Fawr, in the wild landscape that now forms the western, less-frequented corner of the Brecon Beacons National Park. It was there that he died and, as far as we know, he only left his native Wales when, at the time of the yellow plague, he went with several of his fellow countrymen to Brittany, where he stayed with Samson (28 July) at Dol.

Teilo was venerated throughout South Wales, and after his death, Llandeilo Fawr, Penally (in Pembrokeshire) and Llandaff Cathedral all claimed his body. Miraculously it became three bodies in the course of one night, so enabling a set of relics to be enshrined at each place; but Llandaff still claims his tomb. A hundred years later, the gospels of St Chad, written in south-west Mercia, were claimed as the property of a church dedicated to St Teilo, and a marginal note claimed that the saint founded the monastery of Familia Teliavi, a settlement that has still to be located.

Throughout the Middle Ages, oaths were taken on St Teilo's tomb, which was opened in 1850, revealing the record of a previous opening in 1736, when the remains of a staff and chalice had been discovered. Teilo's cult tells us nothing of the man, who in Brittany was to become the patron saint of horses and apple trees. I am grateful to Patrick Thomas, Rector of Brechfa, in the forests to the west of Llandeilo Fawr, for the legend that Teilo, in company with David (1 March) and Padarn (15 April), went on a pilgrimage to Jerusalem. There, Teilo humbled himself before the Patriarch of the Holy City by choosing a chair of cedar wood rather than a throne of precious metals. There is a political element in this tale, for by making their pilgrimage to Jerusalem, the three saints, or their biographers, were declaring an independence from Rome; and by seating themselves on the elaborate thrones, David and Padarn were demonstrating something about the hierarchy of the Welsh church, which Teilo's devotees turned to their advantage as a demonstration of the saint's humility.

TRUMWIN 10 February

In 681 Trumwin was consecrated Bishop of Abercorn on the Firth of Forth, and so, according to Bede, had spiritual dominion over the 'Picts who were then subject to English rule'. From there, in the autumn of 684, he accompanied King Egfrid of Northumbria and 'other devout and distinguished men' on a voyage to Inner Farne where they managed to persuade Cuthbert (20 March) to abandon his solitude and accept the administrative powers and duties of a bishop. The following year, the Picts rose up against the English, who were defeated at the Battle of Nechtansmere. Trumwin fled south to the double monastery of Whitby where the holy Elfleda was Abbess. He died there in 704 having lived, Bede tells us, 'to the benefit of many besides himself'.

CAEDMON 11 February

Although Caedmon was not a Celt, he had the Celtic gift of poetry, and is included here because his talent was encouraged by Hilda (17 November). He was a lowly lay-brother working as a herdsman at her monastery at Whitby, and a man who kept alone because he found it hard to join in any community singing or verse-making. When the other brothers came together to make music and poetry, he found himself tongue-tied and crept away to the cattle byres. It was there one evening that an angel appeared to him in a vision and told him to sing of the creation. In this way he received the God-given gift of language, composing poems on the Genesis stories which included the great hymn to the creation, part of which is quoted by Bede:

> Praise we the Fashioner now of Heaven's fabric,
> The majesty of his might and his mind's wisdom,
> Work of the world-warden, worker of all wonders,
> How he the Lord of Glory everlasting,
> Wrought first for the race of men Heaven as a rooftree,
> Then made he Middle Earth to be their mansion.

Bede, who gave this extract in Latin (the translation comes from the Penguin Classics edition of Bede's *Ecclesiastical History of the English People*), confessed that this was only a general sense of Caedmon's original, for 'verses, however masterly, cannot be translated literally from one language into another without losing much of their beauty and dignity'.

GOBNET   11 February

To escape a family feud, the young Gobnet left her home in County Clare to live on one of the Aran islands. There she had a vision in which she learnt that this was not to be her final home, but that she must settle in the place where she found nine white deer grazing. So she came back to the mainland and journeyed to the south-east, until she saw such a herd near Dungarvan. There she founded a nunnery, overlooking the sea from the slopes of the Monavillagh Mountains, at the place which now bears her name, Kilgobnet. She was to become renowned for her skill as a bee-keeper.

ETHILWALD   12 February

A disciple of Cuthbert (20 March), Ethilwald became Prior and then Abbot of Melrose, and was eventually consecrated Bishop of Lindisfarne. He died in 740, and when Holy Island was threatened by Viking raids, his relics, with those of Cuthbert, were carried on to the mainland and through Northumbria.

MODOMNOC   13 February

Like Gobnet (11 February) a famous bee-keeper, Modomnoc was born into the princely house of Ireland, being a descendant of Niall of the Nine Hostages. From Ireland he went to Wales, where he became a pupil of David (1 March); and as a monk he concentrated on gardening, cultivating both flowers and vegetables as well as looking after the bees. When the time came for him to return home to Ireland, a swarm of his bees followed him to his ship; so he took them with him and made hives for them near his monastery in Kilkenny.

Brigid's Feast

I should like a great lake of finest ale
For the King of kings.
I should like a table of the choicest food
For the family of heaven.
Let the ale be made from the fruits of faith,
And the food be forgiving love.

I should welcome the poor to my feast,
For they are God's children.
I should welcome the sick to my feast,
For they are God's joy.
Let the poor sit with Jesus at the highest place,
And the sick dance with the angels.

God bless the poor,
God bless the sick;
And bless our human race.

God bless our food,
God bless our drink,
All homes, O God, embrace.

Traditional

BERACH   15 February

A descendant of Brian, Prince of Connaught, Berach was taken
for the church by the priest who baptized him and who promised
his mother that God would provide sustenance for the child
Accordingly, when the baby cried for the breast, the priest gave
him his ear to suck, and a copious flow of honey came from it.
When Berach grew up, an angel guided him to Glendalough and
there he settled, and two stories are told of his time there. The
first concerns a wolf who devoured the calf of one of the monks'
cows, who lowed so piteously in her distress that Berach bade the
wolf come and suckle her in the place of her lost calf.

The second took place in mid-winter, when a young lad fell sick,
fretting and crying that only apples could cure him. Berach was
told to go and find apples, an impossible task at that time of year;
but knowing that nothing is impossible to God, he set out. The
first tree he came to was a willow, and when he blessed it, it broke
into bud and blossom, and these ripened into little red apples.
Moreover, the snow melted beneath the tree and sorrel pushed
its way through the ground. Berach cut some of this, picked the
apples, and took both to the sick boy, who soon recovered.

LOMAN AND FORTCHIERN   17 February

Jocelyn, the biographer of Patrick (17 March), claimed that he based his work on an Irish life of the saint written by Loman, Patrick's nephew, the son of his sister Trigridia. Loman is said to have accompanied Patrick on his mission to Ireland and to have brought the boat that carried them across the Irish sea up the River Boyne to Trim. There Fortchiern, a local prince and son of a Scottish princess, heard him singing the psalms and was so enchanted by the sound that he came to the boat to receive the faith. His conversion brought a crowd of people to Trim to be baptized, and eventually Patrick set up a church at that place.

FINTAN OF CLUAN-EDNECH   17 February

A disciple of Columba of Tir-da-Glas, Fintan became Comgall's teacher, having established his own monastery in east Meath in the middle of the sixth century. There he instituted a very strict regime for his monks who followed a vegan diet, tending their own vegetables. Disturbed by the criticism of his severity, he was told in a dream that the following morning he would meet the person who would tell him how to cope with the confusion that his critics caused him.

The first person he met that day was a dumb man, who received the gift of speech for long enough for him to tell Fintan that although the path he followed was the right one for him, he should take account of those whose needs led them to a different way of life. So when a deputation approached him, he found himself ready to mitigate the severity of his rule for his monks, although he continued to adhere to it strictly himself. Fintan's good sense and charity is exemplified in the way he dealt with the Celtic cult of the severed head. He did this, not by any miraculous event but by giving proper burial to the heads brought to him by warring tribesmen, and praying for the souls of the slain 'since the principle parts of their bodies rest here'.

FINAN OF LINDISFARNE   17 February

Sent from Iona to succeed Aidan (31 August), Finan was Bishop of Lindisfarne for ten years from 651, and worked closely with

Oswiu, King of Northumbria. He built the wooden church on
the island, a building that was covered with the long strands of
marram grass that grows on the sand dunes of Holy Island. He
sent out missionaries to the Saxons of Mercia and Essex, and was
praised by Bede (27 May) for his great virtue, humility, love of
poverty, and diligence in the work of the church.

COLMAN OF LINDISFARNE   18 February

In 661, Colman, an Irish monk from Iona succeeded Finan (17
February) as Bishop of Lindisfarne, and so it fell to him to be the
main speaker for the Celtic church at the Synod of Whitby. When
Wilfrid triumphed and the Roman rites were instituted, Colman
withdrew to Iona taking thirty Anglian monks with him as well
as the relics of Aidan, Finan's predecessor. From Iona they went
west to Ireland, and Colman established a monastery at Inishbofin,
but because of sad disputes between the native Irish and his Anglian
followers, the latter were settled separately at Mayo.

ODRAN   19 February

According to the life of Patrick (17 March) written by Jocelyn,
Odran drove the cart in which the saint travelled. Realizing that
there were threats against the life of his master and that enemies
were lying in ambush for him, Odran begged Patrick to drive the
horses, while he took the saint's place in the cart. So it was, and the
murderers deceived by the change, thrust their spears into Odran,
whose soul, Patrick saw, was carried by angels into heaven.

   Because of the similarity of the name some people have identified
Odran with Odhran (27 October). There is a link in the fact that
both men voluntarily sacrificed themselves in order to clear the
way so that the work of a greater saint could be carried out.

OLCAN   20 February

Born posthumously to an English woman who had married in Ireland, Olcan was destined to become a bishop in Antrim. The story
goes that when his mother heard of his father's death, the news
threw her into a coma so deep that she was thought to be dead and

so she was buried. Fortunately a nobleman passing the grave heard
the wailing of a baby, and when the tomb was opened, the mother
was indeed dead, but the baby lived to be brought up by the nobleman who had heard his cried. Eventually Olcan was ordained but,
according to Jocelyn's *Life of Patrick*, he came into bad favour with
the apostle of Ireland for promising eternal life, in an attempt to
gain peace, to a pagan chieftain who was tyrannizing the church.

ELWYN   22 February

An Irish monk, who came to Cornwall with a group of saints
which included Breaca – said by the sixteenth-century John Leland
to have been a nun at a convent founded by Brigid (1 February) –
Elwyn is remembered at Portleven at the mouth of the Hayle River.
That place derives its name from Porth Elwyn, so indicating where
the saint made his landing.

The Blackbird of Derrycairn

> Stop, stop and listen for the bough top
> Is whistling and the sun is brighter
> Than God's own shadow in the cup now!
> Forget the hour-bell. Mournful matins
> Will sound, Patric, as well at nightfall.

Version – Austin Clarke

FEBRUARY PILGRIMAGE

Penmon Priory and Seriol's Well

A Candlemas pilgrimage on Anglesey will take you to Seriol's Well, set in a small enclosure near the site of the thirteenth-century Augustinian priory and the church of Penmon. It was here, near the crossing to the island of Priestholm, also known as Puffin Island, where Seriol founded his monastery, that the holy man spent long, solitary hours in prayer. The place still retains much of the peace that Seriol gave it.

You can reach Penmon by the coast road from Beaumaris, or you can walk there by the footpaths as shown on the map. If you take the latter course, you will pass the former site of a tenth-century cross (now in the Priory church). It is carved with the figure of the third-century Antony of Egypt, the first hermit saint and taken as a model by the monks and abbots of the Celtic church.

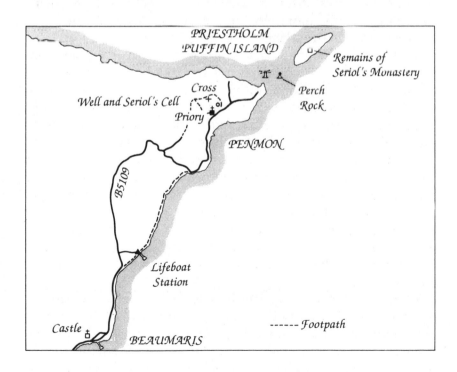

 # March

The Desert

Whenever Easter falls, Lent comes in March. It is a good month then, as we think of the forty days that Christ spent fasting in the wilderness, to visit, if we can, some of the places where the saints of the Celtic church withdrew to confront their own demons. As I write, I am thinking especially of the cave on the stony beach on the northern shores of the Solway Firth, where Ninian retired from the stress of organizing monastic life and running his collegiate church of Candida Casa, the present day Whithorn. Here, lapped by the cold waves but freed for a while from the pressures of human demands, he endured the elements and confronted the more terrifying depths of his own soul.

I think too of the island of Inner Farne, where you are able to land at this time of year if you take the boat that plies from Seahouses when the weather is not too rough. Later in the year when the puffins and other sea-birds are nesting you can sail round the island, but not step on to it. Cuthbert would have approved this restriction, for he loved all creatures and took especial care to protect the speckled eider duck which swim in these waters.

On the island you can walk about the place where Cuthbert spent so many solitary months and where a tiny chapel was built in the Middle Ages, beside the site of the guest hut which Cuthbert put at the service of the pilgrims who dared the journey across the wild sea to visit him. Even when he was on Lindisfarne itself, the high tide Holy Island, he would withdraw from time to time to a little rock by the abbey, which is cut off twice a day by the encroaching sea.

Visiting such sites of ancient hermitage, we can appreciate the quests of the followers of the saints in the fifth and sixth centuries, who might undertake grave hardships and face life-threatening dangers in their frail craft in order to learn wisdom from the holy men. Their journeys were in the same tradition as those undertaken by the early Christians in the Egyptian desert, who sought out the first hermits, hoping for 'words to live by'.

We all need, from time to time, to undertake such quests as those travellers were set on, or those who in later years sailed northern seas to sit at the feet of Celtic holy men who had modelled themselves on a way of life three or four centuries old. The curse that blights so much of life today arises from a sad paradox. We are continually hearing of the isolation of life in the cities, and those who have experienced it know that this is no exaggeration. Yet few of us have the time, imagination or energy to make a place of positive, deliberate solitude either inside or outside our homes. Only a very fortunate few are able to lay claim to a piece of land, however small, in which to spend long days alone as Thoreau did at Walden Pool. But the example of Antony of Egypt, the first Christian hermit, who in the late third century lived alone for twenty years on the deserted hill fort of Pispar, is still an example which can inspire us to seek out some solitude for ourselves. A corner of the house, a special part of a public park, a garden, a woodland, any of which can be regularly visited alone and made our own, can become small hermitages in which solitude can be realized and felt as a blessing; and where, when we are ready for it, our worst fears can be faced and dealt with. It is important that we should love the place we choose, as the Celtic hermits loved their places of hermitage, rejoicing in the songs of the birds, the movements of the trees, and the constantly changing shapes of the clouds. It is also important that we do not look on our times of solitude as an escape from or an alternative to our lives as members of a community of families, friends and neighbours.

In this respect too we can find models coming from Egypt through the Celtic church in the monastic settlements. In Egypt, these monasteries, developed during the fourth century, were places to which Christians could withdraw to live together, working and praying for the good of the world. Both men and women formed such groups; and these became models for the double monasteries, usually ruled over by an abbess, which were to become familiar institutions of the Celtic church.

The early Celtic monasteries evolved directly from that set up by St Martin at Tours, which Ninian is said to have visited before founding his own Candida Casa. They also owed much to the druidic schools, many of the early converts to Christianity being former Druids, and the practice of founding a school or college in conjunction with the larger monasteries became common.

For the monks, the routine of monastic life followed the Benedictine practice of dividing the day between prayer, study and work based on the monastic vows of poverty, obedience and stability. Some of the sites in which these monks lived have been preserved for us because of the extreme isolation of their setting. The most famous site, consisting of the oratory church and the individual beehive huts for the monks, is high up on Skellig Michael, a rock 8 miles (13 km) off the coast of Kerry. I have yet to go there, and meanwhile as I visit other less spectacular places I have the memory of the beehive huts of the Coptic community on the roof of the Church of the Holy Sepulchre in Jerusalem to remind me of the origins of the Celtic monastic settlements.

It was a Celt, born in Scythia in 360, who first brought monasticism out of Egypt to Gaul. John Cassian found himself so in tune with the small monastic groups that he visited in Nitria and Scete to the west of the Nile Delta, that he set up two such monasteries near Marseilles. One of them was on the island of Leirin. It was an example that the founders of the Celtic monasteries often chose to follow, the surrounding seas cutting them off from the temptations of worldly concerns even more surely than the desert sands isolated the Egyptian monks they were emulating.

It is usually agreed that the apostolic number of thirteen was thought to be the ideal size for starting a monastic settlement, although this could grow into a community of several hundreds. That was how the monastic colleges evolved, and how in the seventh century the two valleys of Glendalough in the Wicklow Hills became almost a monastic city. Here the monks lived under the direction of the Anamachara or soul friend (Periglowr in Wales). These were older or more experienced monks, more counsellors and spiritual directors than confessors, and a long-standing relationship of this nature was of the greatest importance to the monks.

Even so, the pressures of monastic life, especially for those in authority, were so great, that, as we have seen, the abbots and priors would often follow the Egyptian model and withdraw into isolation from time to time. Ninian possibly learnt this safeguard from Martin of Tours, who had his own hermitage in the cliffs of Marmoutier, close to the monastery that he founded about the same time that John Cassian made his settlement in the south.

Work in the monasteries was largely a matter of looking after the primitive buildings and tilling the soil, work which the hermits also undertook for themselves, for they insisted on being self-supporting. Doubtless the monks of Whithorn had to bring food across the stony beach to Ninian's cave but that was an exception. I think that even in such inhospitable surroundings, that fifth-century saint might have cultivated a small patch by the flower-filled banks of the stream that runs down through the woods to the sea, a few hundred yards from the cave, and possibly he sometimes caught the salmon, which still provide a good harvest in the Firth.

Like Antony of Egypt, who claimed on his death-bed that he had never eaten anything he had not grown, the Celtic monks, whether in a monastery or a hermitage, had this robust determination to care for their own needs. So, even as hermits, their life of prayer and study was interspersed with the work of their vegetable plots, a necessity which kept their spirituality fully earthed in a way that few of us in an urban society can easily appreciate. We may make a symbolic token of it, however, if only by growing a few herbs in pots on the kitchen window sill. If you do that, enjoy it, but do not be fooled. In our technological urban society our urgencies are elsewhere. The parsley and the leaves of basil will not keep us from starvation, but tending to their growth will, at least, give us a link with the forces of nature of which we are a part, and which ultimately remain outside the province of human technology, however sensitive and sophisticated.

In the fifth century, the cultivation of food, particularly in these northern isles, demanded back-breaking relentless toil. To get oneself out into the fields and turn the earth on a cold, windy March day, demands willpower, so it is small wonder that the particularly British heresy of Pelagianism should have arisen out of a confusion between the grace of God and the will of man.

Pelagius was a fourth-century Briton, who went to Rome to promulgate his teaching that salvation lay largely in our own hands, and that by acts of will and self-control we could make ourselves into better people, more acceptable to God and to our fellows. This doctrine was initially accepted by Jerome, and even by John Cassian who wrote of it in his thirteenth conference, a manuscript that was to be omitted from the canon of his writings when the fallacy of the teaching became apparent. For the idea of the supremacy of the will was seen to be in opposition to the teaching that only by the grace of God could the wills of mankind be activated for good.

No doubt a certain amount of politics was involved, especially at a later date when some leaders of the Church in Rome set themselves up as interpreters of that grace. It was a matter far greater than the dating of Easter and the style of the tonsure, and it was this that really motivated the Roman faction at the Synod of Whitby in 664. For a full account of this synod, which was fully documented by Bede, and which marked the end of the Celtic Church as a separate entity, see my *Celtic Alternative* (Random Century, 1992).

However, as we shall see as we come to look at the life of David of Wales, the balance of grace and will was a matter of great concern to the leaders of the Celtic church. In the early fifth century, the leaders of that church asked for help from across the Channel in order to refute the heresy of Pelagius. Germanus, Bishop of Auxerre, who undertook that task, made several visits to Britain; and he must have shown the full power of heavenly grace when, by arranging for a great host to chant hallelujahs, he managed to turn back an army of Picts and Saxons, without a drop of blood being split.

February was the time to think of the feminine aspects of Celtic spirituality; now in the month of Mars and the butting ram of Aries, it is fitting that the male characteristics of strength of will and determination should be in our minds. We will see how these considerations influenced the lives of many of the saints whose festivals we celebrate at this season; and how, tempered by grace, they could bring about results as strong, and ultimately as peaceful as the hallelujah victory.

DAVID   1 March

Three places in the southern half of Wales are particularly associated with that country's patron saint. They are: the district of Henfynyw, near the coast of Cardigan Bay to the east of the River Aeron, where the young David is said to have been taught by Paul Aurelian (12 March); the westerly tip of north Pembrokeshire, an area of windswept heathland then known as Menevia, where David was supposed to have been born and where he established his main settlement in the valley, which was later to be filled with the medieval splendour of a cathedral built in his honour; and Llanddewi Brefi, a small town near Tregaron. There, at a place crossed by three Roman roads, a church tower was raised in the twelfth century on the hill where David refuted the Pelagian heresy at a synod of his bishops.

Despite the gentle nature of David's much-quoted dying words: 'Noble brothers and sisters, be joyful and keep the Faith and persevere in the little things you have heard and learnt together with me', he kept a regime of strict austerity. No wine was drunk in his monastery, and although his monks were allowed a little fish, the main staple of their diet was vegetables, and they lived largely on the wild leeks, which have since become the national emblem of Wales. On such a diet they had to work hard, for David decreed that no draught oxen should pull their ploughs. Much of their days were spent in silence.

March they say goes out like a lion, and there is reputed to have been a great storm at the time of David's birth; it comes in like a lamb, with a gentle stillness, and so it was at the time of his death. I have been in Wales on St David's Day, when a cold clear sun shone above a frozen landscape, whose white frost was punctuated by mounds of dry bracken. It seemed a fitting image for David's love of simplicity, a honing down to make space for the emergence of a new spring. The weather that I experienced was also a fitting image for David's work in providing a still centre of peace in a world torn by tribal strife, for the legend goes that on the 1 March that he died, in 588, a brilliant sun shone on his mourning followers. Yet I am uneasy; on the 17th of this month we celebrate the feast of Patrick, and it concerns me that these two Lenten saints so notable for their opposition to the doctrines of Pelagius, may simply be as historical as our King Arthur, an amalgam of emissaries trained by Roman prelates to refute Celtic heresies.

Destiny of the Britons

Their Lord they shall praise,
Their language they shall keep,
Their land they shall lose
Except wild Wales.

Sixth-century, by Taliesin

CHAD 2 March

Ironically enough I have no doubts about the historical authenticity
of Chad, although I did have to ask myself if the first Bishop of
Mercia really belongs in a calendar that concentrates on the Celtic
church. Yet this Saxon, who held a bishopric and who lived and
worked for eight years after the Synod of Whitby, had spent part
of his youth in Ireland and later became a disciple of Aidan (31
August) through whom he was imbued with the spirit of Iona.
Like his great master, he refused any special honours and insisted
on making his extensive travels on foot rather than on horseback.
While he was Abbot of Lastingham, Oswy, King of Northumbria
sent him to Canterbury to be consecrated Bishop of York.

   Chad was actually consecrated bishop by Wini of the West
Saxons, a prelate who still adhered to the Celtic calculation
for the date of Easter. That gave the Northumbrian Wilfrid,
Rome's champion at the Synod of Whitby, a splendid excuse
to oust Chad from the See when he returned to Northumbria
from the Continent in 669. Chad responded to his dethronement
with characteristic humility, declaring himself only too willing to
resign an office for which he had never considered himself worthy,
although in obedience he had undertaken it.

   Chad's worthiness for the post of bishop was proved again
when Wulfhere, King of Mercia asked for a bishop to be appointed
to his newly Christianized kingdom. Theodore, Archbishop of
Canterbury, appointed Chad to that See, and during the remaining
three years of his life, Chad established his bishopric from Lichfield
and settled a monastery close by. He died in 672 and a hundred
years after his death, the monks of Lichfield transcribed a gospel
book on the Celtic pattern. For centuries it was associated with
the shrine of Chad, and it can still be seen in the chapter house
of his cathedral.

JOAVAN 2 March

This Irishman, who became a monk at Landevenic in Brittany,
was a disciple of Paul Aurelian (12 March). He died in 562 and
his tomb is at Plougen.

Non with the baby David

WINWALOE 3 March

Founder of the monastery at Landevenic in Brittany, Winwaloe was trained by Budoc (8 December) and for some time lived as a hermit on the Breton island of Tibidy. Monks from his monastery at Landevenic set up foundations in Cornwall, and in the Middle Ages his cult spread widely throughout Britain. In Norwich he even joined David (1 March) and Chad (2 March) in a weather rythme:

> First comes David, then comes Chad,
> Then comes Winnol, roaring like mad.

NON 3 March

In a field on the eastern side of a small rocky bay to the south of St David's in Pembrokeshire, you will find the ruins of a small chapel, said to mark the place where the young Non gave birth to David (1 March). For centuries pilgrims landed here and prayed in Non's chapel before journeying on to David's shrine.

According to Rhigyfarch, who wrote the life of David at the end of the eleventh century, Non or Nonnita, a maid of Pembrokeshire, was raped by Sanctus, a prince of Cardigan. As a result she bore a son, who thus had an earthly ruler for father and a holy nun for mother. So Non, partly because of the accident of her name, came to represent the mother of the church in Wales, where she was beloved as a healer and peace-maker and as one who believed, in the words attributed to her, that 'There is nothing more stupid than argument'.

She is connected with both Cornwall and Brittany, and some sources claim that she fled to France with her infant son. In Cornwall she is honoured at the church of Alternon (the altar of Non) for it was here, according to William of Worcester writing in 1478, that the saint was buried. There is also a figure of her in the Breton church of Dirinon, about a mile (1½ km) from which there are two wells, one dedicated to Non and the other to her son, David. Here a miracle play was annually performed in her honour. At Alternon and also at Tavistock in Devon her feast is also celebrated on 15 June.

Canon G.H. Doble suggested in his *Saints of Cornwall* that the real Non was not David's mother at all, but a monk or missionary who was David's companion. This man, Nonna, is remembered

Non's Well

at Penmarch in the south-west corner of Brittany, and shares the
Alternon feast day of 15 June.

PIRAN (PERRAN)   5 March

The sands along the coast from Perran-zabulo in Cornwall stretch
far out towards the sea. Buried beneath them there is an oratory,
believed to have been founded by this monk from Ireland or Wales,
who landed here in the fifth century. Piran was to become the
patron of the Cornish tinners, and until the Middle Ages, when
the sands covered the site of his hermitage, hundreds of pilgrims
walked towards the sea to pray at his shrine. The oratory was
excavated in 1858 but, in order to preserve it, it has been covered
over again now, and marked by a concrete cover, which is also
beginning to disappear beneath the sands. You can find the place,
however, for a tall Celtic cross stands beside it.

Like many another saint who crossed the Bristol Channel to
Cornwall, Piran is said to have sailed the sea on a millstone, a
miraculous voyage apparently; but I believe that the story simply
refers to the ballast which held his light craft steady in the water.

The Cornish tinners, celebrated his festival with great fervour.
The 1759–64 cost-book of the Great Work Mine in the parishes
of Breage and Germoe lists an allowance of a shilling to the men
and sixpence to the boys paid out at Perran-tide. At that time,
Canon Doble (*see* Bibliography) records, a man 'of unsteady step
and festive appearance' was called a Perraner.

Piran was remembered in Wales in a chapel dedicated to him
near Cardiff Castle where, as Gerald of Wales tells us, Henry II
heard Mass on Low Sunday, 1172. He is sometimes confused with
the Irish Ciaran of Saighir, whose feast also falls on this day, and
who is honoured in Brittany. Canon Doble describes a wayside
stone shrine to him beside the road between St Pol-de-Leon and
Lesneven.

Nicholas Roscarrock, a Cornishman writing in 1580, tells us
that in his life-time, 'Piran's reliques were wont to be carried upp
and down in the country upon occasion'.

CIARAN OF SAIGHIR   5 March

Saighir, near Birr in County Offaly in the centre of Ireland, was a prehistoric sacred site, one of the places in which a perpetual fire burnt for centuries. It may well be that there was a Christian community here long before Patrick (17 March) came to convert the Irish. It was to become the burial place of the Kings of Ossary, for it was here that Ciaran from west Cork, who became a Christian during his travels on the Continent founded his monastery. Its ruins still survive.

Ciaran is said to have had a particular affinity with wild animals and stories tell how he enlisted the help of a wolf, a badger and a fox in the building of his monastery and the cultivation of the site.

Near Fastnet rock, at the extreme south-west corner of Ireland, is the island of Cape Clear. This may have been Ciaran's birthplace, and the ancient ruined church which stands there is believed to mark the place where he founded a second monastery.

BALDRED   6 March

Bass Rock stands off the coast from Dunblane in Lothian, near to the birthplace of Kentigern (13 January). In the eighth century it was the home of the hermit Baldred, who came here from Tyningham in Northumberland. He is said to have prayed successfully for the removal of a dangerous reef that lay between the mainland and his rocky island home, for it moved out of the way of shipping to its present site, where it is known as St Baldred's Rock.

Baldred must also have had a settlement on the mainland, for at Whitekirk a well dedicated to him attracted many pilgrims throughout the years, and was renowned for its powers of increasing fertility.

Because of the location of his hermitage, Baldred is sometimes confused with the earlier, seventh-century, Baldred who was Kentigern's disciple and companion.

BILFRITH   6 March

When the monks took Cuthbert's body and the treasures of
Lindisfarne on to the mainland, to keep them out of the way
of the Viking raids, they eventually arrived at Chester-le-Street.
There, the priest Aldred added a colophon to the manuscript
of the famous Lindisfarne Gospels recording for posterity the
fact that the book's leather cover, adorned with gold, silver and
precious gems, had been worked by the anchorite Bilfrith. Alas,
it is lost to us now, but Bilfrith's reputed relics were taken to
Durham and there his feast was celebrated jointly with that of
Baldred.

ENODOC   7 March

Almost buried in the sands of the Camel estuary in north Cornwall
is the nineteenth-century church of St Enodoc, immortalized in
a poem by Sir John Betjeman, whose mother is buried there.
The present building replaces a much earlier church, known
as Sinkinnery, which had almost completely disappeared and
where it had become quite impossible to hold services. Excavations have shown however that the original church had an
oval, Celtic churchyard, and Celtic remains dating from the
third and fourth centuries have been found in the neighbouring
dunes.

   Enodoc was probably associated with Bodmin Priory, and is
believed to have come to the coast as a hermit, settling by the
fresh-water spring which was discovered when the flagstones by
the rood screen of the nineteenth-century church were found to
be constantly damp.

SENAN   8 March

Born near Kilrush in County Clare, Senan, who died in 544,
was the founder of several monasteries, the best known being
on Scattery Island near his birth-place. His bell shrine is in the
Royal Irish Academy in Dublin. He is also associated, perhaps
erroneously, with Sennan, near Land's End in Cornwall, said to be
the site of a monastery whose learning was acclaimed throughout
the Celtic world.

CONSTANTINE   9 March

Converted by Petroc (4 June), Constantine, a Cornish king with a Roman name, went to Ireland to become a monk after the death of his wife. There he worked in a humble capacity tending the water mill, a position he had to forgo as soon as his identity was discovered. He then went to join Columcille (9 June) in Iona, and was martyred on one of the missionary journeys from that island. He is venerated in Scotland, Wales and Cornwall, where his name is remembered in the parish 5 miles (8 km) to the south-west of Falmouth and in a bay near Padstow.

Pangur Ban

I and Pangur Ban my cat,
'Tis a like task we are at:
Hunting mice is his delight,
Hunting words I sit all night.

Better far than praise of men
'Tis to sit with book and pen;
Pangur bears me no ill will,
He too plies his simple skill.

'Tis a merry thing to see
At our tasks how glad are we,
When at home we sit and find
Entertainment to our mind.

Oftentimes a mouse will stray
In the hero Pangur's way;
Oftentimes my keen thought set
Takes a meaning in its net.

Ninth-century

OENGUS THE CULDEE   11 March

Author of the earliest martyrology, Oengus, a leading member of the sect who referred to themselves individually as *Céli Dé*, a servant of God, lived as a hermit before joining the monastery of Tallacht near Dublin. There for some years he worked with Maelruan (7 July). He died in 824.

MURA 12 March

The London Wallace Collection has the bell shrine of this early seventh-century Irish abbot, while his crozier is displayed in the Royal Irish Academy. He founded the monastery of Fahan (County Donegal) on the shore of Lough Swilly to the north-west of Londonderry. The tall cross that marks that site is now a national monument.

PAUL AURELIAN 12 March

E.G. Bowen, a professor of geography at the University of Aberystwyth, who traced the journeys of the Welsh saints in his *Britain and the Western Seaways*, described the travels of this monk from the west of Wales, who left his native land as a *perigrino pro Christo*. Professor Bowen conjectured that Paul Aurelian made his first landfall on the islands of Ushant and that he probably made a settlement on the Ile de Batz, off the north coast of Brittany, before finally establishing his monastery on the site now known as St Pol de Leon. There he was consecrated bishop, and there he died at the age of 104.

As a young man, together with David (1 March), Samson (28 July) and Gildas (29 January), he was a disciple of Illtyd (6 November), attending the monastic college at Llantwit Major (Llanilltud Fawr) on the coast of Glamorgan. Paul Aurelian's eleventh-century French biographer tells us that he was not yet sixteen when he decided to live as a hermit. If this is so, he is probably the same man as the Welsh Paulinus, who lived for some years as a solitary near Llandovery before founding a monastery at Lladdeusant on the edge of the moorland surrounding the stark cliffs of the Black Mountain.

The reports of his piety and holy life spread so widely that King Mark of Cornwall sent for him to preach to his people. This led him to spend some time in that land before, in response to a message given to him by an angel in a dream, he crossed the sea to Brittany.

A Hermit's Song

My heart stirs quietly now to think
of a small hut that no one visits
in which I will travel to death in silence.

I will have no ease nor long lying,
but short sleep, out on the edge of life,
and early waking for penance and long prayer.

Hardly a mile from this pleasant clearing
is a bright spring to drink from and use
for moistening measured pieces of bread.

For all my renouncing and sparse diet
and regular tasks of reading and penance
I foresee only delight in my days there.

Version – James Simmons

The Monastic Scribe

A hedge before me, one behind,
a blackbird sings from that,
above my small book many-lined
I apprehend his chat.

Up trees, in costumes buff,
mild accurate cuckoos bleat,
Lord love me, good the stuff
I write in a shady seat.

Early ninth-century

PATRICK   17 March

One may speculate as to whether Patrick was an actual individual
or a team of missionaries sent by Rome to refute the heresy of the
learned, fourth-century monk, Pelagius. Of Patrick we know next
to nothing although he is said to have written accounts of his own
missionary life; but of Pelagius, we are assured by his detractor and
contemporary Orosius that he was a huge and proud Goliath; and
Jerome writing in 414 (Pelagius lived until 430, Patrick is said to
have died in 461) declared that the heretic walked 'at the pace of
a turtle' having been made 'heavy by Scottish porrige'.

Both Pelagius and Patrick appear to have been born in western Britain, somewhere between the Bristol Channel and the
Solway Firth, most probably in the region we now know as
Cumbria. Both left written works behind them. Pelagius, the
apostle of the moral will, commented on Paul's famous passage in
I Corinthians 13, 'You follow charity with every effort, strive after
it because it is within your powers'. Like the Druids, according
to M. Forthomme Nicholson (writing in the *Introduction to Celtic
Christianity* edited by James P. Mackey), Pelagius believed that
everything in nature was good, but that it depended on the will of
man for it to remain good; and Mr Nicholson likens the teaching
of that burly, forthright monk to the creation teaching of Peter
Abelard in the Middle Ages and to that of Matthew Fox in our
own time. By contrast, Patrick, or the missionary group that he
epitomizes, was the prophet of grace and the need to obtain it by
harsh penance.

According to a life of the saint, written two hundred years after
his death, he was the son of Calpornus, a deacon and grandson of
Potitus, a priest. At the age of sixteen he was captured by pirates
and sold as a slave into Ireland, and there he tended his master's
beasts on the hills of County Antrim. Much later, having managed
to escape back to the mainland, he returned as a missionary to the
country of his enslavement. On that second visit to Ireland, he
established a church above Strangford Lough, and there in 433, on
25 March (Easter Saturday), he lit the paschal fire. In doing so, he
followed the custom of the druidic Fire Festival in which every fire
in Ireland had to be extinguished at the time of the spring equinox
and relit from a new fire kindled on the low hill of Tara.

Patrick came prepared for his new mission, having first gone to
Auxerre, where he was ordained by Amator, the predecessor of

Germanus (31 July). This ensured the orthodoxy of his teaching. When seven years of missionary travel in Ireland were completed, Patrick is said to have spent the whole of Lent on a mountain in County Mayo overlooking Clews Bay, and now known as Croagh Patrick. Each year, on the last Sunday of July, there is a pilgrimage to this place attended by thousands of people, while in Donegal particularly severe penances are undertaken on St Patrick's Island in Lough Derg. This ascetic tradition of Ireland's national saint is complemented by the traditional hymn of protection, the 'Breastplate of St Patrick'. Although the lines of this well-known hymn probably belong to the eighth century, they epitomize the Celtic tradition of the *caim*, the imaginary circle infused with the power of God, which a person could draw around themself and which would ensure protection on a journey.

The writings attributed to Patrick and said to have been written towards the end of his life are a *Confession* and a letter full of anger against the Scots and Picts. Both are written in the Latin of the Bible before Jerome prepared his translation from the Hebrew, and the *Confession* has a blessed note on interior prayer: 'And another time I saw him praying within me, and I was as it were within my own body'.

Patrick is said to have died at Saball near Wicklow on 17 March, at the very place where he landed in Ireland to begin his missionary journey.

The Muse of Amergin

I speak for Erin,
Sailed and fertile sea,
Fertile fruitful mountains,
Fruitful moist woods,
Moist overflowing lochs,
Flowing hillside springs,
Springs of men assembling,
Assembling men at Tara,
Tara, hill of tribes,
Tribes of the sons of Mil,
Mil of boats and ships,
The high ship of Eire,
Eire of high recital,
Recital skilfully done,
The skill of the women
Of Breisi, of Buagnai;
That haughty lady, Eire,
By Eremon conquered,
Ir and Eber bespoken:
I speak for Erin.

Version – John Montague

FINAN OF ABERDEEN   18 March

A disciple of Kentigern (13 January), Finan worked in Anglesey before coming to Scotland about 573. He founded several Christian settlements around Aberdeen.

Poem for the Ideal Hermitage

I wish, O Son of the living God, O ancient, eternal King,
For a hidden little hut in the wilderness that it may be my dwelling.

An all-grey lithe little lark to be by its side,
A clear pool to wash away sins through the grace of the Holy Spirit.

Quite near, a beautiful wood around it on every side,
To nurse many-voiced birds, hiding within its shelter.

A southern aspect for warmth, a little brook across its floor,
A choice land with many gracious gifts such as be good for every
  plant.

This is the husbandry I would take, I would choose, and will not hide
  it:
Fragrant leek, hens, salmon, trout, bees.

Raiment and food enough for me from the King of fair fame,
And I to be sitting for a while praying God in every place.

Irish, ninth-century, translated by Daphne D. C. Pochin Mould

CUTHBERT   20 March

When Bede (27 May) wrote his life of Cuthbert, he vouched
for its authenticity, declaring in his preface that he had written
nothing without ascertaining the facts and talking to people who
had actually known the man. From Bede we learn that it was
while the young Cuthbert was with some shepherds (probably
on the Lammermuir Hills of the Border country) that he had an
angelic vision, coinciding with the death of Aidan (31 August).
This convinced him to follow the vocation of that beloved founder
of the Abbey of Lindisfarne.

Cuthbert's first step was to become a monk at the monastery
of Melrose, where the Irish Boisil (7 July) was abbot. From there
he was sent with the monk Eata (26 October) to the monastery at
Ripon. It was while he was serving as guest master there that he
first became aware of the bitter divisions between the Celtic and
the Roman churches. The dispute was to concern him for the rest
of his life, as he gave himself wholeheartedly to healing that split
so that both traditions could work together in authentic harmony.
It was not an attitude that the Roman faction, headed by Wilfrid,
then Abbot of Ripon, could tolerate, and Cuthbert soon found
himself back at Melrose, where he tended Boisil during his
last days.

After Boisil died, Cuthbert became Prior of Melrose; but when
Eata was appointed Abbot of Lindisfarne, he took Cuthbert with
him as Prior, and it is with that Holy Island that the saint
is primarily associated. In the Celtic tradition, Cuthbert had
always managed to spend some time as a solitary hermit and by
contrast also to travel widely throughout the surrounding country,

talking to the people he met along the way. On Lindisfarne he made his hermitage on the tiny Thrush Island, a rock on the beach below the Abbey that gets surrounded by water at high tide.

For longer solitary periods, he retired to the island of Inner Farne for months at a time. If you land there now, you can climb up to the little chapel where the wise man had his oratory, his cell and a shelter for visitors who crossed the wild sea to consult him.

At Thrush Island and on Inner Farne, Cuthbert befriended the eider ducks, who are still known as Cuddy's chickens, from the saint's pet name. Another story about his affinity with animals comes out of his concern for the unity of the church. When he went to talk with Wilfrid's supporter, Ebba (25 August), at her Abbey of Coldingham, to try and work out some suitable compromises, the sea otters came to warm him and dry his feet after he had spent an entire night wading in the cold sea, praying and reciting the psalter.

After the Synod of Whitby in 664, at which the supremacy of the Roman church was confirmed, Cuthbert felt an increasing need for retreat, and in 676 he relinquished his post as Prior of Lindisfarne and withdrew to Inner Farne. He was to live there for the best part of ten years. Bishop Trumwin of Abercorn (10 February) was to be instrumental in bringing Cuthbert back into the world. After the saint's death, Trumwin told Bede a story that Cuthbert had confided to him concerning his youth. It dealt with a time when he was playing rather over-boisterously with the local lads. A three-year-old child interrupted the game, upbraiding Cuthbert for his wild behaviour and addressing him as 'Most holy priest and bishop'. Cuthbert must have recalled that incident when Trumwin, accompanied by King Egfrith of Northumbria, sailed over to Inner Farne to persuade the hermit and former prior to become Bishop of Lindisfarne. It was a post that Cuthbert reluctantly agreed to fulfil.

As bishop, in great contrast to Wilfrid, he always took thought for the poor, and according to Bede 'He strictly maintained his old frugality and took delight in preserving the rigours of the monastery against the pomp of the world.'

For nearly two years Cuthbert gave his services as bishop to the people of Northumberland. Then, knowing that his end was near, he retired once more to Inner Farne. There he died on 20 March 687. A hundred years after his death and burial by the altar in Lindisfarne Abbey, the whole coast was threatened by

Viking pirates. The monks, fearful that Cuthbert's relics would be desecrated, carried his body around the north-east from one safe haven to another, until they finally laid it to rest in Durham Cathedral. It was to be moved again in the eleventh century when the Cathedral was rebuilt, and lies now in the shrine behind the high altar there.

Sayings Attributed to Cuthbert

1. Let us knock at our Lord's gate with prayers.

2. Keep peace with one another and Heavenly charity.

3. Why should we become drowsy in so much sloth, and not seek by some means or another the way of salvation?

4. Maintain mutual accord with other servants of Christ.

5. Despise not those of the household of faith, who come to you seeking hospitality.

HEREBERHT OF DERWENTWATER   20 March

A priest and hermit, who lived on an island in Derwentwater, Hereberht made a practice of journeying east each year to visit Cuthbert (20 March) on Lindisfarne or Inner Farne. Late in 686, it was Cuthbert who made the journey, travelling west for the ordination of deacons in Carlisle. So Hereberht took that opportunity to talk with his soul friend nearer home. When Cuthbert told him that this was the last time that they would meet on earth, for he knew that his own death was near, Hereberht implored him to pray that 'they might journey together and see God's glory in Heaven' for he dreaded being left alone on earth. That prayer was answered, as Cuthbert was assured that it would be. Shortly after their meeting, Hereberht fell ill, and he died on 20 March 687 at the same moment that Cuthbert's spirit left his body.

ENDA   21 March

A pioneer of Irish monasticism, Enda was trained at Whithorn in Galloway. When he returned to Ireland, he founded his own monasteries in the Boyne Valley before finally settling on Inishmore, the largest of the Aran Islands, where you can still see the ruins of his settlement. Cieran of Clonmacnoise (9 September) was one of his pupils, and Brendan (16 May) consulted him before he set out on his long voyage, according to the tenth-century life of that wandering saint.

Enda died in 530 and is buried at Tighlagheany on Inishmore.

The Baptism by the Knee-woman

In name of God,
In name of Jesus,
In name of Spirit,
The perfect Three of power.

The little drop of the Father
On thy little forehead, beloved one.

The little drop of the Son
On thy little forehead, beloved one.

The little drop of the Spirit
On thy little forehead, beloved one.

To aid thee, to guard thee,
To shield thee, to surround thee.

To keep thee from the fays,
To shield thee from the host.

To sain thee from the gnome,
To deliver thee from the spectre.

The little drop of the Three
To shield thee from the sorrow.

The little drop of the Three
To fill thee with Their pleasantness.

The little drop of the Three
To fill thee with Their virtue.

Collected by Alexander Carmichael

GWINEAR   23 March

According to a fourteenth-century life of this saint, Gwinear was
martyred by King Theodric of Cornwall at some uncertain date.
He came to Cornwall with Meriasek (7 June), another saint whose
date is uncertain, although they probably both lived some time in
the sixth century, and worked around Camborne. Later the two
men went to Brittany, and at Pluviguen near Vannes Gwinear
is portrayed in a stained glass window, hunting a stag. That fits
with the story that when Gwinear was out hunting, three wells
sprang from the ground where he struck his lance. One was for
him, another for his dog, and the third for his horse. Perhaps the
miracle was associated with the stag, who is shown with a cross
between his horns, which may have arisen from confusion with
the legendary Eustace, patron of hunters (a saint of unknown date
who is depicted encountering such a stag), or could signify the
saint's encounter with the supreme sacrifice, his martyrdom.

DUNCHAD   24 March

It was in 716, while Dunchad was Abbot of Iona, that Egbert,
a monk of Lindisfarne, came into Scotland to persuade the
community at Iona to adopt the findings of the Synod of Whitby
and to tonsure their hair in 'the symbol of the unbroken crown'.
Bede gives a full account of the success of Egbert's preaching,
but says nothing as to whether Dunchad welcomed the proposed
changes before his death, which occurred shortly after Egbert's
arrival.

DONARD   24 March

A convert of Patrick (17 March), Donard set up a hermitage and
an oratory on the Mountains of Mourne overlooking the present
town of Newcastle. Slieve Donard, which bears his name, is
capped by two prehistoric cairns, indicating that there, as at his
principal church of Maghera in County Down, he made use of an
existing druidic site on which to establish a Christian settlement.
Pilgrimages are regularly made to the summit of Slieve Donard,
and there is a tradition that the saint continues to say Mass there
each Sunday.

Birth Baptism

In name of Father,
                          Amen
In name of Son,
                          Amen
In name of Spirit,
                          Amen

Three to lave thee,
                          Amen
Three to bathe thee,
                          Amen
Three to save thee,
                          Amen

Father and Son and Spirit,
                          Amen
Father and Son and Spirit,
                          Amen
Father and Son and Spirit,
                          Amen.

Collected by Alexander Carmichael

TYFIL   27 March

A nephew of Teilo (9 February), Tyfil is the only child saint that I
have found in the Celtic calendar. He was accidentally killed in the
woods by the banks of the Tywi, beneath the hill to the west of
Llandeilo which now carries the gaunt, medieval ruins of Dynevor
Castle.

GWYNLLYW FILWR (WOOLOS)   29 March

In the sixth century Gwynllyw lived above the marshes to the
east of Cardiff that are now known as the Wentlooge Levels.
According to one account, he wanted to marry Gwladys, one of the
twenty-four children of Brychan (6 April). That lady, according to
the author of the life of the twelfth-century Caradoc, enjoyed 'a
high reputation, was elegant in appearance, beautiful in form, and
wore silk dresses'. Her father, however, refused to give his consent,

so Gwnllyw took the lady by storm, riding with three hundred men to the court at Talgarth to snatch the maiden away.

The couple were eventually converted to Christianity by their son Cadoc (25 September), and thereafter they lived an austere celibate life, bathing daily in the Usk, and establishing a settlement round their oratory on the high ground now known as Stow Hill in Newport. Gwynllyw chose that place for he had been told in a dream to settle where he found a white ox with a black spot on its forehead.

MARCH PILGRIMAGE

Cuthbert's Cave, Northumbria

The rock shelter, known as Cuthbert's Cave, where the saint sheltered when he travelled on his missionary journeys from Lindisfarne, can be reached from the Roman road that runs south from Berwick-upon-Tweed through Lowick. At Holburn Grange, to the east of the road, you come to land owned by the National Trust, and here you will find clear directions for finding the cave. To reach it you will walk along a green lane, and if spring has come early, you will find your path flanked by white violets.

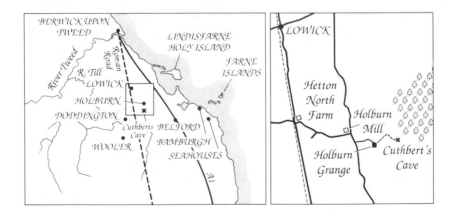

 **April**

Travel and Pilgrimage

A thousand years before Chaucer opened his prologue to *The Canterbury Tales* with a panegyric to the month of April and the stirring in the blood that makes people long to get out on the road, the early Celtic Christians (men and women) set out from Ireland, Scotland and Wales to journey for God. They were emulating Abraham, who left his settled homeland at the command of Yahweh, and like him they made no plans but trusted that God would direct their footsteps. We are told that they even went to sea rudderless, letting the currents, the tides, and the winds take them to a destination known only to God.

In this way they followed the exhortation, which prefaces the life of Columcille in the early medieval *Book of Lismore*, 'to leave their country and their land, their wealth and their worldly delight for the sake of the Lord of the Elements and to go on perfect pilgrimage'. In this way they sought *Tir Tairngiri*, the land of promise. Their journeys can be a model for all our travelling, no matter how prudent it seems to draw direct routes on maps, correlate railway and bus time-tables and schedule ourselves right out of the life of the places we find ourselves in.

Those early Christian travellers, wandering over the country-side, sometimes alone, sometimes with one or two companions, made no such mistake. According to the accounts that we have of their travels, mostly written during the Middle Ages, they often submitted to being led by animals: cattle, deer and oxen, to the places where they were destined to make at least a temporary settlement. For they were always to be wanderers on the face of the earth, often torn as Columcille was with homesickness for their native land, but determined always to go forward into the unknown. These wanderers, *peregrini* as they are often called, loved islands – as we see when we look at the monasteries and hermitages of the Celtic saints. Those who crossed from Wales to Cornwall and thence to Brittany, would settle on one of the thousands of islands that dot that rugged coastline. On some of them you can still find traces of a small, long-ruined chapel dedicated to the saint who once made a temporary home here, before travelling inland to minister to the refugees from the Irish pirates and the ravages of the Yellow Plague which had caused them to set up Britain's first colony across the sea.

You will find similar settlements on the islands off the north coast of Britain. In the western Highlands, I think of Columcille's Hinba, where Ethne, his mother, was buried, and which still serves as a place of hermitage, for those who, like the Jesuit, Gerard Hughes, have courage and faith enough to face the total isolation of life on a small, rocky outcrop; and to wait in trust for the fishing boat to come and collect them on the appointed day.

Emrys G. Bowen, a great Welshman of our own time, who celebrated the wanderings of the *peregrini* in his book *Britain and the Western Seaways* (Thames & Hudson, 1972), quoted the Irish monk Dicuil, who in the first part of the ninth centuries wrote of some islands in the north sea, possibly the Faroes, which the Irish wanderers discovered about 700. 'On these islands' Dicuil wrote, 'hermits who have sailed from our Scotia [Ireland] have lived for roughly a hundred years. But even as they have been constantly uninhabited since the world's beginning, so now, because of Norse pirates, they are empty of anchorites, but full of innumerable sheep and a great many different kinds of sea fowl. I have never found these islands mentioned in the books of scholars.'

Possibly Dicuil was drawing on the Irish *Imrama*, travel tales of miraculous voyages in northern latitudes where whales blow and volcanoes send out plumes of fire and smoke. A slightly more straightforward account comes in Adomnan's life of Columcille in which the writer describes how the saint's disciple, Cormac, 'was under full sail before a southerly wind for a fortnight, holding a straight course to the north, until he had gone beyond the limits of human journeying'. In this way he may have reached Shetland, the Faroes and possibly Iceland. It is reassuring to know, also from Adomnan, that when Columcille visited the court of the Pictish King outside Inverness, he was given instructions for the safety of those of his followers who were setting out to sail in northern waters. But by the time Dicuil penned his *Liber de Mensura orbis Terrae*, in which the Faroes are described, Norse pirates, the Vikings, as we have seen above, had made the islands untenable to Irish Christians.

The wandering Celts went to the north-west as well as across the grey North Sea, for they were in Iceland by the end of the eighth century. Those colonizers were also forced to abandon their cells and hermitages at the coming of the Norsemen, for they too refused to settle down with the violent pagans; but in this case they left behind their heavy handbells that had called the faithful to prayer, as well as their books and croziers, perhaps as intentional proof of their habitation.

The fact that these holy objects were left behind gives us, in any case, another lesson about their mode of travel – the need to journey light. From the Old Testament instructions to Abraham and the people of Israel as well as in Christ's instructions to his disciples, we receive the same message – do not clutter yourself up for a voyage. It seems a hard lesson to learn. The physical impedimenta of our present-day tourists and trekkers is not only troublesome to the travellers themselves but a cause of considerable hardship to porters and Sherpas who struggle with their luggage along Himalayan paths. More insidious, if less physically demanding on ourselves and other people, is the amount of mental clutter that we take on our daily journeys into the unknown. Every day we set out with such trunkfuls of preconceptions, such badly packed, uncomfortable rucksacks of dogma, prejudice and projects that we are blind to new impressions and might as well never get out of bed, let alone travel to unknown countries and experiences.

TEWDRIC   1 April

A sixth-century prince of south-east Wales, Tewdric in old age handed over his temporal powers to his son, Meurig, and sought a life of quiet meditation. When the Saxon hordes pushed westwards across the Wye, he came out of his retreat to aid the Celtic forces, which were attempting to repel them. At the Battle of Tintern in 595, he received a fatal blow on the head, although he was not killed instantly. He was to die at Mathern (*Ma – Teyrn*, the place of the king) a few miles to the south, where the Wye joins the Severn to form the Bristol Channel.

The story of Tewdric's death brings many of folklore's themes together, starting with the one in which a destination is decided by animal instincts: at Tintern, the body of the wounded king was put on a cart drawn by two stags, who eventually stopped at the well, which you will find beside the road that runs under the

Tewdric

motorway from St Tewdric's Church in Mathern by the medieval palace of the Bishops of Llandaff to the village. It was here that the king's wounds were washed and here that he died.

Saints, living and dying, often entrusted their fate to animals in this way, but Tewdric's story has a more ancient connotation. Nennius, a monk from Bangor-is-y-Coed near Wrexham, writing in the ninth century was most probably referring to this well (he calls it Meurig's Well, so confusing father and son) as containing a log which floated on the water and was large enough for men to stand on as they washed their hands and faces. The spring high tides would carry the log away to the open sea where it stayed for four days before returning inland to the well.

It has been suggested that this log is linked to the wooden female fertility figures, representing Nerthus or Mother Earth, which have been found in the Danish peat bogs. Tacitus, writing in 98 CE described the rituals practised by her worshippers in Schleswig-Holstein. He tells us that in the sacred grove dedicated to Nerthus there stood a cart draped with a cloth which only a priest was allowed to touch. He could feel the presence of the goddess in this holy of holies and attend to her with due reverence as her cart was drawn out of the grove by oxen. The oxen took the cart throughout the countryside and wherever it went it spread peace and joy. On its return to the sacred grove, cart, cloth and goddess were all bathed in a secret, secluded lake, a service which was performed by slaves who were immediately drowned when their task was completed. The suggestion has been made in a booklet written by A. R. Utting and published by Mathern Parochial Church Council in 1985 that such a ritual may have existed in south-east Wales into the Christian era. He also suggests that Tewdric the King, with his head wound, somehow became identified with garrotted ritual victims such as the late Iron Age Lindow man, who in addition to having his throat cut, had a fractured skull.

It is certain that Mathern is an ancient holy place. If you cross the lane to the footpath west of the church, you will come to some curious earthworks by Moynes Court. This is certainly not a defensive position for, as at Avebury, the bank is outside the ditch, suggesting that it was a place from which the holy rituals taking place in the sanctuary could be observed. In the sixteenth century, Tewdric's coffin was opened and as Bishop Godwin (quoted in Cox's *Monmouthshire* (1610)) observed, after a thousand years Tewdric's bones were 'not in the smallest degree changed . . .

the skull retaining the aperture of a large wound, which appeared as it had been recently inflicted'. A further excavation took place in 1881, when the skull wound was again confirmed.

For the Wanderer

Give thee safe passage on the wrinkled sea,
    Himself thy pilot stand,
Bring thee through mist and foam to thy desire,
    Again to Irish land.

Live, and be famed and happy: all the praise
    Of honoured life to thee.
Yea, all this world can give thee of delight,
    And then eternity.

Version – Helen Waddell from medieval Latin

GUERYR   4 April

Little is known of this saint, whose shrine on the southern edge of Bodmin Moor was closely identified with that of the ninth-century Neot (31 July), who gave his name to the place. The two saints were said to be buried beside each other, and Asser, the Welsh monk who became adviser to Alfred the Great, claims that the King made a special point of visiting the double shrine.

DERFEL   5 April

In May 1538 the Franciscan John Forest, confessor to Catherine of Aragon, was condemned to be burnt at Smithfield for denying Henry VIII's claim to be head of the church in England. A little before his execution a statue of Derfel mounted on a wooden horse was brought to him. People who like puns say it was because of the Welsh belief that it would ensure a good burning, for the statue was said to have the power to cause fire, and burn a forest down. Others more charitably felt it would ensure Forest's route to heaven for, according to Cromwell's agent at St Asaph, the people believed the statue had the power to save people from the flames of hell.

To that end, on the saint's feast day thousands of people would come to his shrine, prepared to sacrifice their animals to him.

In his youth Derfel appears to have been a soldier, who became an anchorite in the place which now is known as Llanderfel. In the church there his horse stands riderless in the porch looking, as Jan Morris writes in her *Matter of Wales*, 'less like a holy relic than a long-cherished rocking horse from a medieval playroom'. She also quotes the belief that Derfel was one of Arthur's knights. A more reliable tradition would have him become Abbot of Bardsey Island.

BRYCHAN   6 April

Brychan is frequently referred to in this calendar, for he is the legendary King of Powys who gave his name to Breconshire, and whose enormous progeny bore the gospel into the south-west peninsula and Brittany. Accounts vary as to how many children he actually had, one tells us that the number amounted to twenty-eight sons and thirty-seven daughters. Another story runs that, having already fathered several children, he decided to live apart from his wife and so went to study in an Irish monastery. On his return to Wales, God punished him for such 'illicit continence' and twenty-four children appeared at the next birth. However many children there were, they are supposed to have had a reunion on the last day of each year.

The truth behind all this is the fact of a Celtic tribal group, which had adopted the Christian faith, living in Powys and sending both monks and nuns on the journey south from Wales across the the south-west and on to Brittany.

GORAN   6 April

Goran is thought to be the same man as the saintly Vuron, mentioned in a life of Petroc (4 June), and there described by an angel as a hermit 'winning his daily bread by the labour of his hands and never letting his spirit cease from prayer'.

Petroc is said to have sought him out on Bodmin Moor, and although Vuron entertained him with Heaven-sent food, once they had eaten and talked together Vuron withdrew and found a new, more solitary habitation for himself. It seems possible that Petroc did indeed disturb a previous hermit when he journeyed to Bodmin Moor with his twelve companions.

There is still a St Goran's Well in Bodmin churchyard.

BRYNACH   7 April

The rocks of Carningli, the rock of the angels, surmounted by the remains of an Iron Age fort, stand at the western edge of Mynydd Preseli in Pembrokeshire. To the north, the Afon Nyfer joins the sea at Newport after flowing through the village of Nevern, where the sixth-century Brynach made his settlement. A tall Celtic cross still stands in the churchyard there.

Brynach was an Irishman, who left his native country to become a colleague of David (1 March) and soul friend of Brychan (6 April), who was also to become his father-in-law – for although the Celtic church made no insistence on celibacy, Brynach is one of the few whose marriage is recorded. It was indeed one of his wife's kinsmen, Clether, who gave him the land around the banks of the Nyfer on which to make his settlement. This Clether may well have been related to the fifth-century Clutar, who is named in both Irish and Latin ogham inscriptions on the stone preserved inside the church at Nevern, on a window sill at the eastern end of the nave.

Legend has it that Carningli (the rock of the angels) got its name because it was the place where Brynach chose to spend time as a solitary hermit and was granted angelic visions. Perhaps he went there because you can sometimes see the Wicklow Hills from that height, and perhaps he chose to live in a deserted hill fort in order to follow the example of the first Christian hermit, Antony of Egypt, who lived for twenty years in the deserted hill fort of Pispir.

MADRUN (MATERIANA)   9 April

Madrun was the wife of Ynyr Gwent, a fifth-century chieftain of the Silures, who ruled the area around the Roman town of Venta Silurum, now Caerwent, near Chepstow. She fled from the battles between the Celts and Romans in which, according to Nennius, Vortigern was killed. Taking the youngest of her three children with her, she crossed the sea, presumably to the Celtic monastery

Nevern Cross

at Tintagel, where the church is dedicated to her. So is a church
at Minster in the Valency Valley near Boscastle. It is said that she
died there and is buried in the chancel.

For Materiana's church near Boscastle

Minster of the Trees

The Minster of the Trees! A lonely dell
Deep with grey oaks, and 'mid their quiet shade
Grey with the moss of years, yon antique cell!
Sad are those walls: The cloister lowly laid
Where passing monks at solemn evening made
Their chanting orisons; and as the breeze
Came up the vale, by rock and trees delay'd,
They heard the awful voice of many seas
Blend with the passing hymn – thou Minster of the Trees.

The Rev R.S. Hawker

Hymn of St Madryn (Merthiana)

Madryn, Queen, by foeman's hosts surrounded,
Fleeing from Cambria and her native mountain,
Hasted to Botreaux, there the cross proclaiming,
Christ's healing fountain.

Built she her Minster in Valency's Woodland,
By her, they tell, were miracles amazing,
God through her prayers the sick and dying,
To Life upraising.

Now her white bones in Minster lie buried,
While her pure soul in Paradise imploreth.
God of his love to grant this house of worship,
Grace which restoreth.

A.G. Chapman

The Pilgrim's Rune

King of the Elements – Love-Father of Bliss,
In my pilgrimage from airt to airt,
　　　　From airt to airt,
May each evil be a good to me,
May each sorrow be a gladness to me,
　　And may Thy Son be my foster-brother,
　　Oh may Thy Son be my foster-brother.

Holy Spirit – Spirit of Light,
A pilgrim I throughout the night,
　　　　Throughout the night,
Lave my heart pure as the stars,
Lave my heart pure as the stars,
　　Nor fear I then the spells of evil,
　　　　The spells of evil.

Jesu – Son of the Virgin pure,
Be thou my pilgrim-staff throughout the lands,
　　　　Throughout the lands,
Thy love in all my thoughts, Thy likeness in my face,
May I heart-warm to others, and they heart-warm to me,
　　For love of the love of Thee,
　　For love of the love of Thee.

Collected by Kenneth Macleod

PADARN (PATERNUS OF WALES)　15 April

Founder and Bishop of Llanbadarn Fawr, inland from Aberystwyth, Padarn lived in the first half of the sixth century. It is thought that he came north from south-east Wales.

RUADHAN　15 April

Sometimes claimed as one of the twelve Apostles of Ireland, Ruadhan, who founded the monastery at Lorrha by the northern tip of Lough Derg in County Tipperary, was educated at Clonard, like most of the other eleven. He is said to have taken part in a cursing match against the Druids of the royal palace at Tara, and was so successful that the whole building was deserted and soon fell into ruins.

Blessing of the Road

May the hills lie low,
May the sloughs fill up
In thy way.

May all evil sleep,
May all good awake,
In thy way.

Collected by Kenneth Macleod

DONAN AND HIS COMPANIONS   17 April

In 617 the Celtic Easter fell on 17 April, and it was then that Donan and some fifty of his monks were massacred by Viking raiders who attacked their monastery on the Hebridean island of Eigg. Dr D.D.C. Pochin Mould reports that there was a belief that the pirates' raid was instigated by a powerful woman tribal leader, angry that the monks had settled on her sheep pastures. However that may be, the invaders burst in on the monks as they were celebrating Mass in their chapel. Donan asked them to wait until the service was completed, and then begged that he and his companions should meet their deaths in the refectory, so that they might not 'die so long as we remain in the joy of the Lord', but go 'where we refresh our bodies and there pay the penalty'.

Columcille (9 June) had foreknowledge of this evil event, although it took place some twenty years after his own death. When Donan asked the founder of Iona to be his soul friend, he declined, saying that it was not fitting that he should be the *anamachara* of one destined for the red martyrdom.

An Irish Pict by race, Donan began his missionary journeys around Scotland about 580. There are places bearing his name throughout Kintyre and the Outer Hebrides, and until the Reformation his crozier was kept at Auchterless in Aberdeenshire.

MOLAISE 18 April

Molaise was founder of the monastery on the island of Innish-murray in Donegal Bay, whose ruins still stand, and where he is still honoured. He was also known as Laserian and is venerated in Scotland. He is believed to have spent some time as a hermit in a cave on Holy Island off the east coast of Arran. The hagiography claims that he made a penance for his sins and avoided the pains of purgatory by contracting thirty diseases at once. He is believed to have favoured the Roman calculation of Easter; and the medieval life of the saint even claims that he was consecrated bishop in Rome. He died in 639.

As I write, a Tibetan Buddhist Community is trying to raise funds to buy the Holy Island in the Firth of Clyde, and to set up a place of inter-denominational retreat there. In doing so they are inspired by the spiritual traditions of the island associated with Molaise.

BEUNO 21 April

This sixth-century abbot is in many ways the North Wales counterpart of David (1 March). Born and educated on the eastern borders of the Black Mountains, he was given land to establish a *llan* (the Welsh term for a Christian settlement or church) near Clodock. However the Welsh like to say that when he heard a man shouting to his dog in English, he determined to find a place where nobody used the Saxon tongue, so he travelled north-west along roads engineered by the Romans, until he came to the neck of the Lleyn Peninsula. There, at Clynnog Fawr, he established a collegiate church. The sixteenth-century traveller John Leland claimed that Beuno was buried there in the chapel adjoining the church, in which you may still see a stone with an incised cross, said to have been indented by the saint's thumb. A well dedicated to him stands on the south side of the main road going west out of the village.

Beuno was the spiritual guide of his niece Winefride (3 November), and is said to have been the grandson of Gwynllyw (29 March) and related to both Cadoc (25 September) and Kentigern (13 January).

MAELRUBHA 21 April

A descendant of Niall of the Nine Hostages, this Irish prince was born on 3 January 642. He became a monk and at a very early age was made Abbot of Bangor. He resigned that position in 671 in order to embark on a mission to Scotland. Two years later he settled at Applecross (Aper-Crossan, the mouth of the River Crossan), an all-but island cut off from the mainland by high and virtually impassable mountains. Until quite recently, when the coastal road was built, the place could only be approached by water. That was how Maelrubha came there, sailing across from Skye on a stone according to accounts of his life, a piece of folklore which Hebridean islanders well understand as referring to the boulders used to ballast the boats.

From Applecross (a monastery which always maintained a close connection with Bangor) Maelrubha set out on his missions to the Picts. He went as far east as Dingwall; and then set out north across the ancient sandstone mountains and swirling scree of Torridon to Loch Maree, which bears the phonetic rendering of his name. There he set up a monastery on the smallest island of the loch. That densely wooded place had been sacred to the Druids before he came there, and after his death its pagan influences reasserted themselves and became confused with the cult of the saint, for bulls were sacrificed in his honour.

He actually died further to the north at Skail in Sutherland where he had gone on further missionary journeys. The year was 722 and he was eighty. His companions carried his body back to Applecross, and until the Reformation his grave was marked by a cross of red sandstone, although the monastery that he founded was destroyed in the Viking raids at the end of the eighth century. Only two fragments of that cross remain now. They have been placed inside the church, while two round stones in the churchyard mark the supposed site of his grave. They say that anybody taking a little earth from that place can travel as far as they will and always come back safely to Applecross.

The cult of Maelrubha continued until the end of the seventeenth century, and for a further two hundred years his well on the island in Loch Maree was reputed to have the power to cure madness. There are other wells of Maelrubha in the western isles, and you find a Tobermoray (well of Maelrubha) on Skye and on Mull. For centuries his crozier was kept by the Dewar, a guardian of relics, at Balindore (the township of the Dewar) by Kilvary on Loch Etive.

IVO   24 April

One tradition that claims Ivo as a Persian bishop who came to England and gave his name to the village of Slepe (now called St Ives) in Cambridgeshire is contradicted by another, which claims he was a Cornishman who travelled east and died in the settlement that he made near the Fens in 600.

MACHALUS (MAUGHOLD)   27 April

Possibly a native of the Orkney Islands, Machalus, who lived in the fifth century, became Bishop of the Isle of Man. It is said that he began his career as a pirate, and that after he converted and abandoned that life Patrick (17 March) ordered that he make penance for his evil ways and show his faith in the dispensation of God by putting out to sea in a coracle without oars or rudder.

He appears to have been swept ashore on the eastern side of the Isle of Man, where a holy well bears his name. This is in àn area where standing stones signify the presence of megalithic peoples, and where Iron Age tribesmen built the hill fort, which as Professor E.G. Bowen pointed out in his *Saints, Seaways and Settlements* overlooks a natural landing place by the present church which is dedicated to Maughold (the Manx version of his name). That building is referred to in the life of Patrick, which the monk Jocelyn wrote in 1185.

ENDELLION   29 April

One of the daughters of Brychan (6 April) and said to be a god-daughter of King Arthur, Endellion came across the Bristol Channel to Cornwall, presumably spending some time on Lundy Island on the way, for a chapel there by a Christian Celtic graveyard is dedicated to her.

Possibly she then landed at the Celtic monastery of Tintagel, for she is remembered at St Endellion's to the west, just inland from Port Isaac, where there was once a collegiate church. She is said to have lived as a hermit a little to the south of the present village, but to have been buried where the church now stands, for that was the place where the bullocks, pulling her funeral bier, stopped.

APRIL PILGRIMAGE

Tewdric's Well, Mathern

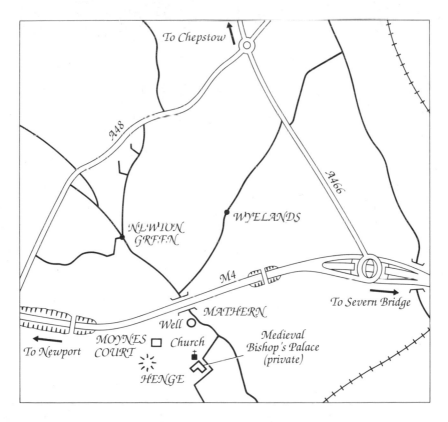

Although it is so near the M4 and the Severn Bridge, the Welsh village of Mathern seems completely remote. If you visit the church, where Tewdric was buried, standing near the remains of a medieval palace of the Bishops of Llandaff (now in private hands), you can make your

way east through the churchyard to the curious earthworks by Moynes
Court. These are thought to be a ritual henge. Mathern's well stands
by the lane that runs north-east out of the village and goes under the
motorway.

Beltaine

May Day
The Start of Summer

 # John

Nowadays we celebrate the feast of St John the Evangelist on 27 December, but until the late Middle Ages his festival was also kept on 6 May, and it seems fitting that we should remember the writer whose words were a glorification of the 'light that darkness could not overpower' during the months of the longest days. Beloved by the leaders of the Celtic church, John was the patron saint of Scotland before St Andrew, and a stone cross dedicated to him was the last relic of Columcille's Celtic church on Iona. This cross, now restored, is part of the fabric of the new abbey.

The eagle, which symbolizes this evangelist in the *Book of Kells*, is a proud bird with heavy wings and coiled tail feathers, his head and beak surrounded by a ringed halo marked with three crosses. At first sight this seems to be a strange creature to represent the author of the gospel of love with whom the Celtic church had such a strong affinity. Yet we know from their penitentiaries, and from the austerity of their lives as monks and hermits, that the love that burned in the hearts of the Celtic saints was constantly demanding, relating to reality with a hawk-like awareness far removed from the woolly, comfortable sentimentality which we too often confuse with love. Yet the eagle is not the whole of the story. There is also a portrait of John in the *Book of Kells*. He sits, a brown-eyed, auburn-haired Celtic figure, holding a book in one hand and looking out from the page with a kindly intensity. He is surrounded by an elaborate frieze, from which disembodied hands appear at each side, feet at the bottom, and what looks like two cowled heads at the top.

John's gospel, written at Ephesus towards the end of the first century, is deeply imbued with Jewish ritual and custom. This affinity would have appealed to the Celtic mind, for the nomadic Israelites, like the tribal Celts, realized God's presence in all creation and had prayers for every occasion, however simple. Above all, John's gospel is imbued with the Holy Spirit. From the very first chapter in which he records the Baptist's confirmation that he 'saw the Spirit coming down on him from heaven like a dove and resting on him', we are aware of the continual presence of the Holy Spirit linking the temporal incarnation of Jesus to the eternal Son of God. The Spirit, often spoken of in terms of the invisible wind, is also symbolized in the Scottish Highlands by the migrating wild grey goose, appearing unexpectedly and with no apparent temporal nesting place. In that way the bird seems to transcend time and space as the dove, in the story of Noah, brought news of peace and promise from the land beyond the veil that separates time from eternity.

The Holy Spirit shines through John's gospel, transforming a historical document into a living, ever-present and insistent message. It was this that made it so beloved of Columcille of Iona; caused Boisil of Melrose to find consolation on his death-bed, when Cuthbert read a chapter of this gospel to him each day; and which inspired Cuthbert's followers, twenty-six years later, to place that same copy of St John's gospel in their beloved bishop's coffin.

 # May

The Care of the Land

Imbolc is the season of light, Beltaine is the time of growth. Yet it is also the time when we are most aware of light for the longest days fall in this season, and this is the time when we are most aware of the dawn. So it is no wonder that the Beltaine Blessing, which Alexander Carmichael collected from the western Highlands should look, at this time, with gratitude on the preservation of:

> Everything within my dwelling or in my possession,
> All kine and crops, all flocks and corn,
> From Hallow Eve to Beltane Eve.

Brigid of the season of light and Columcille whose feast falls during the months of Beltaine, were both looked on as the protectors of cattle, and together with Mary they are often invoked at this season, when the herds start to graze the summer pastures. The Celtic farmers practised transhumance, following their cattle to summer grazing grounds, so that like the Lapps who constantly move after the reindeer herds as they search for moss, their lives were inextricably bound up with the animals they cared for. In the winter they lived in the sheltered valleys beside those beasts who were chosen to be kept alive during the cold, dark months. At the beginning of summer they took those animals up to the hill pastures. In Wales the words *hendre* and *hafod* refer to these winter and summer farms respectively. In Scotland the summer farmstead is a *sheiling*, and so in that same blessing, the 'gay mountain *sheiling*' is specially mentioned:

> What time the kine shall forsake the stalls,
> What time the sheep shall forsake the folds,
> What time the goats shall ascend to the mount of mist.

This link between man and animals, and the earth that sustains them both, is what agriculture should still be about. The American poet, Wendell Berry, who farms in Kentucky, reminds us that 'The word *agriculture*, after all, does not mean "agriscience", much less "agribusiness". It means "cultivation of the land". And *cultivation* is at the root of the sense both of *culture* and of *cult*'; and in all his writing he shows himself constantly aware of the inter-relatedness of the whole of creation. However much these Celtic tribes might fight each other for territory, their rituals and songs demonstrate a similar awareness. It was an attitude which the peaceable early Christian settlements reinforced. Like the Jewish Hasidim of the seventeenth century, they were not pantheists, that is they did not worship nature, but saw the whole world in Martin Buber's terms as 'an irridation of God'.

Such a world view makes man responsible, as Buber explains, for liberating the spark of divinity in all things by 'holding holy converse with the thing and using it in a holy manner'. In order to do that we must have an intense awareness and respect for the present moment for the people and for the animals we encounter each day, for the tools we use, and for the earth we walk on and which produces our food. In this sense the breaking of bread is always a sacrament; and the constant mindfulness of the Buddhists, reflected in the precision of the Celtic farming songs, must take the place of hurry and greed. Christianity today, Berry complains, is not earthy enough. Complaints about our materialistic society are wrongly couched, for our acquisitive consumerism has little respect for matter – even our coinage is alloyed metal.

To be aware of the divinity of creation, is also to be aware of the spirit of evil and destruction that can invade it. Meg Peacock, a former teacher who now runs a smallholding in Cumbria, describes how on those days when nothing goes right 'the animals are bolshie because I'm rubbing them up the wrong way'. Against these destructive spirits which can invade the soul of man and the creation of which he is part, the breastplate or *lorica* of Patrick calls on the protection of all the elements.

> For my shield this day, I call
> Heaven's might,
> Sun's brightness,
> Moon's whiteness,
> Fire's glory,
> Lightning's swiftness,
> Wind's wildness,

Ocean's depth,
Earth's solidity,
Rock's immobility.

Seeing that we are all so involved with each other and with the
whole of creation, it is pertinent to question or even, as Matthew
Fox does, to go beyond the idea of responsible stewardship,
formulated by the Green movement. To be aware of the earth
and all her creatures is to defend them, as we do ourselves, from
the powers of darkness. This means that our involvement has to
go beyond good management into true participation, in a way that
the Celtic farmers understood when they blessed the May-time
shearing of the sheep:

Go shorn and come woolly,
Bear the Beltane female lamb,
Be the lovely Bride thee endowing,
And the fair Mary thee sustaining,
The fair Mary sustaining thee.

BRIOC 1 May

One of the seven saints of Brittany to whom pilgrimages were
regularly made at Easter, Pentecost, Michaelmas and Christmas
throughout the Middle Ages, Brioc was born near Cardigan at the
end of the fifth century. From there he went to Cornwall, where
a parish near Wadebridge still bears his name. Legend has it that
before he embarked for Brittany, when he was well advanced in
age, he was sitting in a chariot chanting psalms one evening when
a pack of wolves surrounded him. His companions fled, but the
wolves stayed around the saint as though asking his pardon. This
miracle caused a passing pagan prince, Conan, to seek baptism,
but Brioc, suspicious of instant conversions told him to wait a
while. As for the wolves, he bade them to depart and hurt no

one, and they 'like meekest lambs went to the wilderness without doing any harm'.

Brioc died in 530, leaving behind a reputation for great charity. He became the patron of purse-makers.

ASAPH   1 May

A disciple of Kentigern (13 January), Asaph worked mostly in north-east Wales, where he became Bishop of Llanelwy (now St Asaph) and most probably founded the cathedral there.

GENNYS   2 May

The parish of Gennys in north-east Cornwall celebrates its titular saint on this date, although admitting that he may well be identical with Genesius (25 August). It is difficult to know whether or not there was a local saint of this name, as so little is known of him either in legend or fact. Certainly he was not, as William of Worcester claimed, an Archbishop of Lismore; and the head relic in the Canons' church at Launceston has been identified as relating to the more authentic Provençal martyr. Gennys presents a challenge, which can only be met by visiting the place said to be associated with him and by researching into local history as an aid to speculation, and as part of a quest which may well prove valuable in itself.

GLUVIAS   3 May

Said to be the brother of Cadoc (25 September) and a nephew of Petroc (4 June), the Welsh Gluvias is patron of the Cornish village of that name near Penryn. He is probably identical with the patron of Coedkernew in Gwent and with the martyred Glivis, mentioned in the *Book of Llandaff*.

HYDROC   5 May

In the churchyard of Lanhydrock between Bodmin and Lostwithiel
in Cornwall, an 8 foot (2 m) Celtic pillar covered in inter-weaving
designs, and which once supported a wheel cross, stands in the
churchyard. It may have been set up by Hydroc, who gave his
name to the settlement and who appears in a Bodmin calendar
of 1478.

EADBERT   6 May

Bishop of Lindisfarne from 688, this Anglo-Saxon saint is included
here because of his devotion to Cuthbert (20 March). Like his
predecessor he needed time alone and spent every Lent as a solitary
either on Thrush Island by Lindisfarne Abbey or on Inner Farne.
He died on 6 May 698 soon after he had made a new shrine for
Cuthbert when the monks had discovered that the beloved body
was untouched by decay, and that even his garments, according to
Bede, were 'not only spotless but wonderfully fresh and fair'. In
the latter part of the ninth century, Eadbert's body together with
Cuthbert's was carried round Northumberland to save the holy
relics from the Viking raids on Lindisfarne.
   In his life, Bede tells us that Eadbert was 'well known for his
knowledge of the Scriptures, his obedience to God's command-
ments, and especially for his generosity in almsgiving. For each
year, in accordance with the Law, he used to give a tenth not
only of all his beasts but also of his grain, fruit and clothing to
the poor.'

INDRACT   8 May

Ina, the eighth-century Saxon King of Wessex, had a vision that
caused him to honour this Irish saint by ordering that his body
be placed in a pyramid of stone on the left side of the altar in the
old wattle church at Glastonbury, which was burnt down in 1184.
St Patrick himself was said to have lain on the right side of the
altar; but in claiming that Indract was one of his disciples the old
chroniclers were suggesting that he followed his teaching and not
that the two men were contemporaries, for a twelfth-century life

gives the date of Indract's departure from Ireland as 689, at least
two centuries after the death of Patrick.

Although we know so little about Indract, he was clearly
an important figure in the Middle Ages and much revered at
Glastonbury. In 1248 a catalogue of the books in the great library
of that Abbey, lost to us at the Reformation, lists a *Life of St Indract*
in good condition. That book has gone, but the saint is mentioned
in an early twelfth-century life, now in the Bodleian Library at
Oxford, as well as in the writings of John, a monk of Glastonbury
who wrote at the end of the thirteenth century. Much later stories
about St Indract appear in an early sixteenth-century collection of
legends of the saints.

From these various accounts we learn that Indract came to
Glastonbury (perhaps on his way to Rome) after making the
voyage, on a 'stone altar', from Ireland to Cornwall, where he
landed at the mouth of the Hayle River. From there he went east
to the Tamar, and at Tamerunta (a place possibly coincident with
Tamerton Foliot to the north of Plymouth) he founded a settlement
at the place where the staff he struck into the ground grew into an
oak tree. In this place he had a fish-pond, which supplied him and
his companions with a constant supply of fresh food, for, so long
as they never took more than they needed, the number of fish in
the water remained constant.

The story of Indract's time in Cornwall substantiated the claims
made by the medieval monks of Glastonbury that Ina had granted
their abbey lands to the west of the Tamar. That is as maybe. The
story that really concerns us is what happened to Indract and his
seven or nine companions (accounts differ as to the number) when
they came into the Somerset marshes. It was there, at Shapwick to
the north of the Polden ridge, that the little band was attacked by a
group of robbers and all but one were killed. The one who escaped
hid himself under a cart, but this was no act of cowardice – the
Celtic church did not believe in unnecessary martyrdom. So the
twelfth-century biographer of Indract can declare of this nameless
companion that he was a true saint. He wrote that Indract's body
was never found but that 'every year on the eighth of the ides of
May when the feast of St Indract, the martyr, is celebrated, during
the night preceding the festival, a pillar of light is seen over him,
rising from earth to heaven; and many people come together to
gaze at the spectacle, but, although they carefully mark the spot
where it is seen, they can never find it again next day, and so the
place where the saint lies is still unknown to anyone'.

Canon Doble suggested that the strange light that was seen was a marsh gas, but the story also accords well with the reports of the lights that were said to have been seen by pilgrims at the site of Indract's lost tomb at Glastonbury.

CATALD   10 May

An Irish travelling monk of the seventh or eighth century, Catald reached Taranto in south Italy, where he made his final settlement. There is a painting of him in the Basilica of the Nativity in Bethlehem.

CONLETH   10 May

In the beginning of the sixth century, Conleth, a skilled metal-worker, lived as a hermit by the Liffy in County Kildare. It was he who made the sacred vessels for Brigid's monastery, and tradition has it that he also fashioned the crozier belonging to Finbar (25 September) which is now in the Irish Royal Academy.

TUDY   11 May

Another of the seven saints of Brittany (*see* Brioc, 1 May), Tudy gave his name to a parish in Cornwall before crossing to the Continent. As a monk and then an abbot in Brittany he made his settlement near Quimper on the little island that bears his name.

COMGALL   11 May

Comgall, disciple of Fintan of Cluain-Edrech (17 February) and teacher of Columbanus (21 November), founded Ireland's greatest collegiate church at Bangor, on the coast to the east of Belfast (not to be confused with the monastery in North Wales founded by Deiniol, 11 September), in 559, and ruled over it until his death some forty years later. The work he did at Bangor, and the standards he set there, lived on, and although the monastery was in ruins by the twelfth century, it is from the library at Bangor that we have much of our knowledge of Irish spirituality.

Comgall prepared for his life's work by spending several years as a hermit on the shores of Lough Erne in the west of Ireland. The regime that he eventually instituted at Bangor, and which was followed by some thirty thousand people, was extraordinarily strict. His followers were expected to be content with one meal a day, taken in the evening; and to obey a discipline which, according to the penitentiaries that have come down to us, was extremely harsh.

The whole regime was made endurable by Comgall's strong belief in the importance of spiritual counsel and direction and the necessity for everyone to be able to rely on a soul friend. When his own director died, he is said to have lamented to his monks in the much-quoted words 'My soul friend has died and I am headless; you too are headless for a man without a soul friend is a body without a head'. He is then said to have asked his monks how he could find a new soul friend. One of them, Molua (possibly the saint whose day we celebrate on 4 August), told him, in an account that has come down to us in a strange mixture of Irish and Latin: 'Take Christ's Gospel and get someone to hold it in front of you and kneel to it until you get a soul friend out of it'. Comgall sent Molua to fetch the gospel, and when he did so, he told him 'Since it is in your hand you shall be my soul friend'. Then, according to the old account, 'Comgall saw a head on everyone and they saw similar'.

Dr D.C.C. Pochin Mould, from whom I gleaned that quotation, asks us to think of Bangor at this time as a place which 'produced a kind of Christian commando, shock troops of Christ, men who in their own lives could give a demonstration to the world around them of the way the devil that is in us all can be controlled and bridled'. It was from the monastery at Bangor that Columbanus (21 November) and Gall (16 October) journeyed south through modern France to Italy and Switzerland; Moluag (25 June) went to Scotland to found the monastery on the island of Lismore; and Comgall himself is said to have visited Columcille (9 June) on Iona, and to have gone with him on the long journey through the Great Glen to preach to the Pictish King Brude in his hill fort palace close to the site of Inverness.

The Rule of St Comgall

Preserve the rule of the Lord;
in this way you will run no risk;
Try not to transgress it
as long as your life lasts.

This is the most important part of the rule;
love Christ; hate wealth;
Devotion to the king of the sun
and kindness to people.

If anybody enters the path of repentance
it is sufficient
to advance a step every day.
Do not wish to be like a charioteer.

Quoted by Esther de Waal in *A World Made Whole*,
(Fount, 1991)

Sleeping Prayer

I am placing my soul and my body
On Thy sanctuary this night, O God,
On Thy sanctuary, O Jesus Christ,
On Thy sanctuary, O Spirit of perfect truth,
The Three who would defend my cause,
Nor turn Their backs upon me.

Thou, Father, who art kind and just,
Thou, Son, who didst overcome death,
Thou, Holy Spirit of power,
Be keeping me this night from harm;
The Three who would justify me
Keeping me this night and always.

Collected by Alexander Carmichael

BRENDAN 16 May

Like Brigid, Brendan is an Irish saint who exists both in time and
in the other world of timelessness. The man, Brendan, was born
about 489 near Tralee on the coast of Kerry. He died sometime
after 570. During that long life he is said to have founded several
monastic establishments, the most important being Clonfert, in a
bend of the Shannon between Lough Derg and Lough Ree.

The legendary Brendan is the hero of an Irish *Imrama*, a tale
of a magical voyage, and as such his journey has become a little
confused, partly I believe because of a similarity of name, with
that recounted in the seventh-century, totally secular, *Voyage of
Bran*. The tradition of Brendan's allegorical and spiral journey is
also rooted in the Celtic Christianity of which he was a part.

According to a Latin text of the saint's voyages, written in
Ireland at the beginning of the ninth century, the inspiration for
setting out to seek the Promised Land of the Saints came from
a certain St Barrind. According to another tradition, Brendan
himself had sight of that Blessed Isle when he looked west
from County Kerry from the mountain which bears his name
and on whose summit the ruins of an oratory beside a well
indicate that this was a place of pilgrimage for many centuries.
There is also a tradition that Brendan planned his great voyage
from the heights of Hungry Hill above Bantry Bay, a place from
which it is possible to see the rock of Skellig Michael, in whose
still existing beehive huts there was in Brendan's time a settlement
of hermit monks.

Having chosen fourteen companions for his adventure, Brendan
and his company fasted for forty days (but for 'no more than three
days at a time' we are assured), as was the custom before the
beginning of any new venture or the establishment of a new
Christian settlement. Brendan then appointed somebody to be
in charge of his monastery and set out westwards to visit Enda
(21 March) in the Aran Islands.

In another version of the story, Brendan received counsel from
the great woman saint, Ita (15 January), who is said to have told
him that he must build a curragh of wood for his journey, for one
made of animal skins would never succeed in such a holy quest.
However, the Latin version of his voyage, as explicit as the biblical
account of Noah's building of the ark, tells us that not only did
Brendan cover the wooden frame 'with ox-hides tanned with the
bark of oak' but that he 'smeared all the joints of the hides on the

Brendan

outside with fat' and moreover that he carried with him sufficient hides for making two further boats together with sufficient fat for their preparation.

Despite the precision of that description, and despite Geoffrey Ashe's highly readable and scholarly version of Brendan's voyages, which he based on the knowledge we have about the daring and astonishingly far-reaching travels of the wandering Celts, Brendan's story remains an allegory that belongs to the world of poetry and myth. It is no more a geographical account than Teresa of Avila's *Interior Castle* is an architectural treatise.

The early compilers of the ever-popular stories of Brendan's voyages were well aware of this. His voyage to the west was a spiral journey that took him seven years; and he revisited the same places each year for the main festivals of the church. On each visit he had learned something from the preceding year's voyaging, and each island he came to taught him some new facet of monastic life.

One actual visit that he is said to have made was to Columcille (9 June). He did not sail to Iona to greet his great contemporary, but went to the remote island of Hinba, 15 miles (24 km) away in the Gavellachs. Here in 1974 another traveller, the Jesuit Gerard Hughes, spent eight solitary days preparing himself to lead an Ignatian retreat; and before he set off for his long walk to Rome, he came back here to camp alone by the island's ruined ninth-century chapel.

(I have drawn on John J. O'Meara's translation of the ninth-century Latin account of Brendan's voyages published by the Dolmen Press, Ireland, 1976.)

CARANTOC   16 May

An Irish monk who came to Wales, said to be an uncle of David (1 March), Carantoc, like many of his sixth-century colleagues, set out for Brittany, travelling through the south-west peninsula on his way there. He is particularly beloved in Somerset, where John Leland reported on his chapel near Dunster in 1540.

The story is that while he was in Cardigan, 'Christ gave him from on high an honorable altar, the colour of which no man understood; and afterwards he came to the River Severn to sail across it, and he cast his altar into the sea and it went before where God willed him to come'. In this account, possibly written by a monk of Dunster, the saint arrived at the western edge of Bridgwater Bay to be greeted by the young King Arthur, who told him that he would show him where the altar had landed if he would tame the dragon that was ravaging that part of the country. When Carantoc undertook that task, the monster greeted him like 'a calf running to its mother. And it bent its head before the servant of God like a servant obeying its master, with humble heart and downcast eyes'. Then, we are told, the holy man led the tamed beast up to the royal hall that topped the hill at Dunster, and thereafter the creature harmed nobody.

Carantoc is also remembered near Newquay in Cornwall where there is a stained glass window depicting the saint.

MADRON 17 May

This sixth-century Cornish saint is remembered at the well and ruined baptistry on the moors of Madron near Penzance, where services are still held and prayer rags tied to branches of the surrounding trees indicate that people still have faith in the healing powers of these waters. The poet, Peter Scupham, who wrote some verses about this well and its pilgrims, envisages the saint standing among the ruins and turning towards the people seeking cures,

> His hands, bleached to sea-air, blessing them
> In the brown habit of his crinkled water

and so makes him part of the regenerative powers of nature.

At one time the waters of this well were thought to be particularly powerful as a cure for rickets, if the afflicted children were dipped into them on the first three Sundays in May, while their silent parents turned to face the sun. The cure was said to have taken place if the waters bubbled as the child was plunged into them.

He Praises the Trees

Huge-headed oak,
you are tall, tall.
Small hazel, pick
me your secret nuts.

Alder, friendly one,
gleam, shine;
you bar no gap
with a toothed thorn.

Blackthorn, dark one,
provide sloes;
watercress, brim
the blackbirds' pools.

Small one, pathway
loiterer, green
leaved berry, give me
your speckled crimson.

Apple tree, let me
shake you strongly.
Rowan, drop me
your bright blossom.

Briar, relent.
Your hooks have fed
content till you
are filled with holy blood.

Church Yew, calm
me with grave talk.
Ivy, bring dream
through the dark wood.

Hollybush, bar me
from winter winds.
Ash, be a spear
in my fearful hand.

Birch, oh blessed
birchtree, sing
proudly the tangle
of the wind.

Version – Robin Skelton

COLLEN   21 May

Patron of Llangollen, Collen, according to a sixteenth-century life of the saint, saved the people of that valley by slaying the evil giantess that threatened their lives and livelihood. As in many tales in which saints are engaged in encounters with dragons and other supernatural, or subnatural, creatures, the giantess killed by Collen may well represent pagan beliefs connected with the destructive element of the mother goddess. This sixteenth-century manuscript also tell us that the saint came to Glastonbury.

HELEN OF CAERNARVON   22 May

The fourth-century Magnus Clemens Maximus, Emperor of Britain, Gaul and Spain, had a dream which led him to marry the Welsh princess, Elen Luyddog. As his wife, she is reported to have organized the building of the Roman roads that traverse Wales from north to south, and which are still collectively known as the Sarn Helen. She is remembered in Llanelan in Gower and at another Llanelan near Abergavenny. She is sometimes identified with Helen, the mother of Constantine (18 August), whose feast is celebrated in the Eastern churches on 21 May.

BEDE   27 May

I have included this Anglo-Saxon monk among the calendar of Celtic saints because it is through his writings in the eighth century that we have much of our knowledge of the Celtic church. It is from him that we have the fullest account of the course of the Synod of Whitby; and, better than that, it is he who penned the most authentic life of Cuthbert (20 March), written in consultation with those, as he claims in the prologue, 'who had lived a long time with the man of God, and who were, therefore, more conversant with the details of his life'.

He was born near Sunderland in 673 at a place which later became the property of his monastery at Jarrow, where he became a monk at an early age, having been schooled there and at Wearmouth from the age of seven. It seems that he never left

Bede's Chair

Northumberland; and he tells us that he devoted his life to the
study of scripture 'amid the observance of monastic discipline and
the daily charge of singing in church'.

In 703, when he was thirty-three, Bede was ordained, and in the
remaining thirty-two years of his life he wrote twenty-five books
on scripture and ecclesiastical history, his best-known work on the
church history of the English people being completed in 713. As
he said himself, 'The rich in this world are bent on giving gold
and silver and other precious things, but I in charity, will joyfully
give my brothers what God has given unto me'. In making such
whole-hearted use of his talent as a historical writer, Bede indeed
gave to his fellow men and women of many generations the
priceless knowledge of their inheritance.

He wrote up to the last moment of his life, being engaged on
his death-bed in 735 in dictating a translation of St John's gospel
to a boy scribe. He is reported to have died as he spoke the final
sentence. He was buried at Jarrow, but in the middle of the eleventh
century his bones were taken to be reburied in the Galilee chapel of
the newly built cathedral of Durham, where they still rest.

BURYAN 29 May

An Irish princess, said to be a friend of Patrick (17 March) and originally known as Bruniec, Buryan came to Cornwall with Piran (5 March), landing on the coast near the present St Ives at a place known as Pendinas. The name of Buryan was current from the sixteenth century and probably derives from the Cornish *hi beriona* (the Irish lady). Her feast is celebrated on this date according to the Irish calendar, but in the Cornish parish near Penzance which is dedicated to her and where the tenth-century King Athelstan built a church in her honour after his successful expedition to the Scilly Isles, her feast is kept on the nearest Sunday to old May Day (13 May).

Hymn for St Buryan

Long years ago across the western water
    Winds brought to this our shore
One glorious within, a king's own daughter,
    To teach our land Christ's law.

The Saints of God His glory are:
    Cantate Domino, 'Alleluia!'

Throughout her days God's little flock she tended,
    A faithful shepherdess,
Leading the sheep her patient love defended
    Against the wilderness.

The Saints of God His glory are:
    Cantate Domino, 'Alleluia!'

From Cornwall

Taliesin's Song

I am Taliesin. I sing perfect metre,
Which will last to the end of the world.
My patron is Elphin . . .

I know why there is an echo in a hollow;
Why silver gleams; why breath is black; why liver is bloody;
Why a cow has horns; why a woman is affectionate;
Why milk is white; why holly is green;
Why a kid is bearded; why the cow-parsnip is hollow;
Why brine is salt; why ale is bitter;
Why the linnet is green and berries red;
Why a cuckoo complains; why it sings;
I know where the cuckoos of summer are in winter.
I know what beasts there are at the bottom of the sea;
How many spears in battle; how many drops in a shower;
Why a river drowned Pharaoh's people;
Why fishes have scales,
Why a white swan has black feet . . .

I have been a blue salmon,
I have been a dog, a stag, a roebuck on the mountain,
A stock, a spade, an axe in the hand,
A stallion, a bull, a buck,
A grain which grew on a hill,
I was reaped, and placed in an oven,
I fell to the ground when I was being roasted
And a hen swallowed me.
For nine nights was I in her crop.
I have been dead, I have been alive,
I am Taliesin.

Anonymous, thirteenth-century, translated by Sir Ifor Williams

MAY PILGRIMAGE

Madron's Baptistry and Healing Well, Madron, near Penzance

Penwith Moor at the south-westerly tip of Cornwall is an area rich in the history of early settlers. Here you will find the ritual stones and cairns of the Bronze Age as well as late Iron Age settlements. Some three hundred years after the village of Chysauster, whose hut walls still stand, was deserted, Madron settled on the moor to the south.

You reach his baptistry and healing well by the lane that runs west from the thirteenth-century church in Madron village. Then you must take a footpath to the north. This path leads first to the ruined baptistry, where you will probably find prayer rags tied to the trees, for many people still value this holy place. From the ruined walls, boards have been laid across the swampy ground to the well: a spring bubbling up in a pool. When rickets were rife, parents hoped to protect their children from the deformity by dipping them in these waters during the first three Sundays of May.

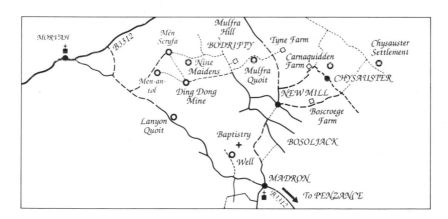

 **June**

Healing

A people conscious of the unity of all creation was also necessarily aware that sickness whether in nature or the individual body cannot be compartmentalized. The whole person has to be treated even if specific symptoms may respond to particular cures, and it is reasonable to suppose that the Celtic Christian settlements went beyond our concepts of the holistic health of the individual to consider the health of the whole of human society. Indeed, now that we live in a world whose advanced technology has not only brought about amazing surgical and medical cures for many conditions, but has also introduced terrible new diseases through wanton interference with the natural order, we too are beginning belatedly to realize that the well-being of each one of us is closely linked to the whole of society and to the health of the planet.

Rachel Carson's *Silent Spring*, published in 1962 long before the disaster of Chernobyl, warned us of the threat that atomic radiation posed to our whole genetic heritage; and in another context listed the horrifying increase in childhood cancers since the beginning of the twentieth century. From such universal disasters and their attendant individual tragedies, it may seem trivial to turn to those plants whose natural healing properties were known to the followers of the Celtic church and to the medieval Hildegarde of Bingen and are still widely used by healers today. I have chosen to consider healing in June because this is the time when many such healing herbs are best gathered.

You will not find many references to specific properties of particular plants in the Celtic songs – there is no herbal that I am aware of – but the Celts went further in their belief in the potency of herbs than we do, for they believed that some of them could act as a protection against unearthly evil. The belief that the rowan, or mountain ash, could save people from witchcraft was current in Wales until the eighteenth century, when the cattle drovers wore a sprig of the tree in their smocks as they set off at this time of year on their long journey to the English grazing grounds. And in this month, when we celebrate the feast of Columcille, it is good to find the leaves of St John's Wort, beloved by this saint and named after the evangelist nearest to the heart of Celtic spirituality. This is one of the few plants to be referred to by the crofters from whom Alexander Carmichael (see Bibliography) collected poems. He was given a plucking hymn for it:

> I will cull my plantlet,
> As a prayer to my King,
> To quiet the wrath of men of blood,
> To check the wiles of wanton women.

The healing and protecting powers of the plants was always felt as a gift from God, and Esther de Waal in *A World Made Whole* quotes the song of a Hebridean woman who had cured herself of leprosy, to express this conviction. Above all, healing of disease was inextricably linked to the healing ministry of Christ, many of the accounts of the cures he wrought being taken from the apocryphal gospels which had reached the early Celtic church from Egypt and North Africa. Among these cures is the one that the infant Christ wrought for the woman who had a cancerous tumour on her breast 'as large and as red as a rose', and who came to the Holy Family while they were fugitives in Egypt.

With the sense of timelessness that made Brigid Mary's midwife and wet nurse to Jesus, the stories of Christ's healing powers are felt to be ever present. Esther de Waal quotes the case of a woman who sets out to heal blindness and who will start off by saying a 'Hail Mary', 'with the lips of her mouth and the cord of her heart', before placing a cross on the blind eye. Then, as Jesus did, she would spit in the palms of her hands and cup them over the diseased eye in the name of the Trinity.

Her words and ritual confirm Wendell Berry's belief that 'Healing is impossible in loneliness, it is the opposite of loneliness. Conviviality is healing. To be healed we must come together with all the other creatures to the feast of Creation.' The lives of the saints that we shall look at during this most convivial month, when people come together as they work out of doors, even now chatting to neighbours over garden fences, and for centuries working together at the vital task of hay-making, reinforces the conviction that we are all bound up in creation.

No wonder then that for centuries people came to be healed at the shrines of saints, whose lives had been in harmony with all creatures.

RONAN   1 June

A ninth-century Cornish monk, Ronan travelled to Brittany, it is supposed in order to escape Viking raids. In France he became a hermit, making his settlement in an area surrounded by holly. He is said to have died on a Maundy Thursday and to have been placed on an ox cart so that the animals could determine the place of his burial. They took him through the Nieve Forest until they came to a stopping place. There he was buried, and in the fifteenth century the great church of Locronan, which houses the saint's granite tomb, was built there.

Every six years his 'pardon' is celebrated by the people of Locronan. Known as *Le grand Trouménie* (the 'Trô-Minihy' or 'Tour of the Refuge'), this Breton pardon, which centres on the mountain within the parish land, covers a distance of 10 miles (16 km). It is hard going and quite unlike any of the other pardons, which make no such strenuous demands; for although the Breton festivals, which have been celebrated in their present form for nearly three hundred years, have been described as vestiges of the feasts of the dead and are deeply religious occasions, the penitential demands are not very severe, and are always lightened by evenings of feasting, dancing and singing.

It is claimed that this unusual venture is partly a propitiation for the sin of Kébèn, a farmer's wife, who tried to seduce the saint. She was so infuriated and embittered by his rejection that when he died she hit out viciously at one of the oxen drawing his body and dislodged a horn; nor was that enough for she hit again at the corpse and marked the face. The pardon culminates beside a nineteenth-century statue of Ronan at the Plac-ai-C'horn, where the horn that Kébèn struck off in her wrath fell to the ground. It is high on the mountain-side, and another story is that this was the place where the oxen stopped for a few minutes so that the saint could take one last look at the countryside he loved.

GWEN TIERBRON, WHITE OR CANDIDA   1 June

If the reports that Gwen Tierbron was the mother of Winwaloe (3 March) are correct, she lived in the late fifth century. She is known as the three-breasted (usually the mark of a witch or a woman with supernatural powers) because she is so depicted in Breton folk art. As *gwen* is the Welsh for white, she has also been identified with the mysterious White or Candida buried at Whitchurch Canonicorum in Dorset. It was once suggested that White, whose feast also falls on 1 June, was a man, Albanus, a Saxon companion of St Boniface of Crediton. But when the coffin there was opened in 1900, the bones of a forty-year-old woman were discovered.

KEVIN   3 June

Our knowledge of Kevin comes from the lives of the saint written three centuries after his death, largely for the purpose of increasing the power and prestige of the monastery that he founded by the two lakes of Glendalough in the Wicklow Hills. Yet the man that emerges from those hagiographies and the words and miracles that have been ascribed to him take me, at any rate, to the heart of that aspect of early Celtic Christianity which is so fundamentally in tune with the harmony of nature. In that context the story of the blackbird nesting on the saint's hands outstretched in prayer does not seem too bizarre a parable. Nor is the story of how the young Kevin, coming to Glendalough to settle by the upper lake in the valley, was accompanied by an angel as he followed the pass through the Wicklow Hills. As they went the Angel cleared the way for him and blessed the trees in the woods they went through.

It is good that there are trees still in the place where he made his hermitage, on a spur of rock above the waters of the upper lake on the site of a Bronze Age barrow. Nearby is the *Teampul na Skellig*, the church of the rocks, at the place where Kevin probably had his oratory.

Glendalough was to become one of the most powerful Irish monasteries of the early Middle Ages. In the ninth century Oengus the Culdee (11 March) described the farmlands in the valleys of the two lakes as 'multitudinous Glendalough'; and it was not long before seven pilgrimages to this site were reckoned to be as powerful as one to Rome. Yet even now, its peace having been assailed by the lead-miners of the nineteenth century and the

tourists of the twentieth, the verses composed about Glendalough
for the tenth-century life of Kevin still ring true:

> A glen without threshing floor or corn rick,
> Only rugged rock above it,
> A glen where no one is refused refreshment,
> The Grace of the Lord is there.

Kevin is said to have visited Cieran (9 September) at Clonmacnoise;
but apart from that his whole long life appears to have been centred
in this valley. The stories have it that he was 120 years old when
he died in 618.

BREACA   4 June

An Irishwoman who was one of Brigid's nuns, according to notes
on her life discovered by the sixteenth-century John Leland, Breaca
founded the Cornish church of Breage, 3 miles (5 km) west of
Helston. It was there that the lost life of this saint was once
housed.

PETROC   4 June

Sometime in the sixth century, Petroc, said to be the son of a Welsh
king, was sent to Ireland for his monastic training. Later he crossed
the Bristol Channel from South Wales, landing at Haylemouth on
the north Cornish coast. He was to become the best-loved saint of
the south-west.

At Padstow (Petroc's Stowe) where he founded his own monastery, you can still see the Celtic wheel-cross outside the south door
of the fifteenth-century church; and by the gate to the south-east
of the churchyard there is a stone stump on which faint markings
can be detected. It is said to be the remains of the cross that once
stood at Petroc's monastic gateway.

When the monastery at Padstow had been established for some
thirty years, Petroc founded a nearby inland settlement in the valley
where Little Petherick is now. In the lives of the saint that have
come down to us that place is called Nanceventan, and we are told
that a mill and a chapel were built there.

In his old age, Petroc set out with twelve disciples to live as a
hermit on Bodmin Moor, settling himself in a beehive hut by the

Petroc

river, and leaving his companions to form a small community on a nearby hilltop. No one knows quite where that was, but I like to think that the tiny, hilltop monastic settlement may have been on Rough Tor, on whose northern slopes there are signs of a Bronze Age village and whose summit still bears traces of a medieval chapel. To the south of that hill you will see Fernacre stone circle and to the east of the stones the deserted farm of Fernacre. There, by the stream that runs out of Rough Tor marsh, you will find a stone beehive hut with a beautifully domed, corbelled roof. The sheep were using it for a shelter when I was last there, and it may well be a medieval construction or belong to an even later date. Sabine Baring-Gould, that great Victorian parson, squire and prolific amateur archaeologist was sure that it was a Bronze Age dwelling. For myself, I would be happy to place it in the sixth century, and imagine Petroc living and praying here. This view is shared by Dom Julian Stonor who describes this hut in the *Downside Review* (LXVI 1948) and claims it as 'one of the oldest Christian holy places in England'.

Perhaps it was at this place that Petroc especially enjoyed the close affinity with wild creatures that he is credited with in many of the stories about him and which is exemplified in later images of the saint with a stag which he is said to have saved from the hunt. A more far-fetched story about his time on Bodmin Moor concerns his dealings with the spirit of the tyrannical Jan Tregeagle, who has been identified with a particularly harsh seventeenth-century landowner of that name. For eternal punishment that man's ghost was doomed to bail out the waters of Dozmary Pool with a cracked limpet shell, until Petroc (possibly wishing his beloved moor to be free of the damned soul) changed his punishment and sent the wretched spirit to sweep the sands of Looe estuary instead.

Petroc was buried at Padstow, but his relics were taken to Bodmin in the reign of Henry II. It was there that nineteenth-century excavators discovered a head reliquary composed of an ivory casket of intricate Islamic craftsmanship.

Dedications to Petroc are common throughout the south-west – there are eighteen in Devon alone. Furthermore it is very possible that many churches dedicated to St Peter after the Roman triumph at the Synod of Whitby, may once have been venerated for their association with Petroc.

There was a Guild of St Petroc for skinners and glovers in Bodmin until the end of the sixteenth century, and there were many legends about the saint in the area. One of them concerns a storm at sea, when a boat crewed by men of many nationalities was on the verge of shipwreck. The Cornishmen on board cried out for Petroc's help. He appeared to them in an alb carrying a censer with which he censed the ship. As he did so the storm ceased.

EDFRITH   4 June

The Saxon Edfrith, who was Bishop of Lindisfarne from 698, is included in this calendar of Celtic saints because of his reverence for Cuthbert (20 March) and his devotion to many of the traditions of the Irish church. He has been called the 'first personality in English art history' on account of his work as scribe of the Lindisfarne Gospels, which he undertook in honour of Cuthbert, and which he lavishly adorned with Irish geometric designs. He restored Cuthbert's oratory on Inner Farne; and his relics together with Cuthbert's and Eadbert's (6 May) were taken throughout Northumbria in the late ninth century.

JARLATH   6 June

A disciple of Enda (21 March), Jarlath came from a noble Galway family, and is said to have been one of the teachers of Brendan (16 May). He is believed to have been Bishop of Tuam to the north-east of Galway town and a shrine was kept in his honour in a chapel there until 1830.

GUDWAL   6 June

Claimed as the first Bishop of St Malo, Gudwal is also honoured at Finstall near Worcester, suggesting that he came from the Welsh borders before crossing into Cornwall, where he is remembered at Gulval, on his way to Brittany. When he first came south, he lived as a hermit on one of the islands of Morbihan.

MERIASEK   7 June

Possibly of Welsh origin, Meriasek was Bishop of Camborne in Cornwall during the sixth century. He is the subject of a Cornish miracle play, *Beunaus Meriasek*, which was revived in Redruth in 1924. An excerpt from this play, relating to the saint's search for drinking water near his Cornish settlement, is given in the Penguin *Celtic Miscellany* (1971). Here it is suggested that Meriasek actually came into Cornwall from Brittany 'across the sea, as God would instruct me'. At least we know that while he was in Brittany he founded a monastic settlement near Vannes.

COLMAN OF DROMORE   7 June

There was a Scottish cult of this sixth-century bishop who worked in County Down, Ulster, for he is said to have been born across the water in Kintyre, the kingdom of Dalraida. He was probably one of the teachers of Finnian of Moville (10 September).

COLUMCILLE   9 June

Generally known as Columba, the Latin rendering of his name, Columcille (the dove of the church) was born Colum MacFhelin MacFergus by Loch Gartan in Donegal on 7 December 521. The day was a Thursday, and that is why for centuries Thursdays were considered sacred to this beloved man of God, and a particularly propitious time for starting any undertaking. His birthplace, now named Glencolumcille, is a centre of pilgrimage.

He came of royal lineage. His mother, Eithne, was a daughter of the royal house of Leinster and his father was the great-grandson of the notorious Niall of the Nine Hostages, who died in 427 having ruled Ireland for twenty-seven years. A ruthless pirate, Niall is said to have been responsible for the raid on the west coast of mainland Britain in which the young Patrick (17 March) was captured.

At the age of nineteen, having decided to enter the monastic life, Columcille became a disciple of Finnian of Moville (10 September) and later of Finnian of Clonard (12 December). In 546, at the unusually young age of twenty-five, he founded his own monastery at Derry, now the city of Londonderry, then an oak grove by the sea, which had once been a Druid sacred site. Columcille revered the trees and it is said that he changed the original plan of his monastery's oratory at Derry so that no trees would have to be felled to make a space for it. In one of his many poems he claimed that he was more afraid of the sound of an axe in Derry woods than he was of hell itself.

His love of books and writing, and his particular enthusiasm for transcribing copies of the gospels and the psalter eventually caused his exile from his beloved Derry. What is reckoned to be the first copyright dispute took place when Columcille, apparently without permission, copied a psalter belonging to Finnian's monastery at Moville. The High King of Ireland, before whom the case was tried, decided that Finnian's rights must stand, but Columcille, filled with the hasty temper of his pirate ancestor, refused to abide by that judgement. Gathering his friends around him, he attacked the King near Sligo, a violence which caused him to be exiled from his native land, and only the intervention of Brendan of Birr (29 November) saved him from being cut off from the church. Seeking the advice of his soul friend, a hermit of Lough Erne, he was told that he must win as many souls for Christ as had been lost in the battle that he had caused.

With twelve disciples he set out from Ireland in 563 and came to the holy island of Iona, on which there was already a small Christian community. Here he set his last and greatest monastery, and here according to Bede (27 May) his successors were 'distinguished for their purity of life, their love of God, and their loyalty to the monastic rule'.

Dr D.D.C. Pochin Mould has described Columcille as a poet, Scottish Nationalist and politician, as well as priest and saint. Certainly he wrote many verses and hymns in addition to the three hundred gospel books that have been accredited to him; his mission to the Picts included political arrangements for the well-being of all Scotland; and he acted, as the Druids had done, as adviser to the Scots/Irish Kings of Dalraida.

In all these activities his strength and energy were tempered by gentleness, love, good sense and above all, joy. Adomnan (23 September), his biographer and successor as Abbot of Iona, writing about a hundred years after Columcille's death on Saturday 9 June 597, describes a man 'gladdened in his inmost heart by the joy of the Holy Spirit'. And according to Bede's report of the dispute at the Synod of Whitby, Colman (18 February), then

Abbot of Lindisfarne, who pleaded the Celtic case, claimed that he would never cease to emulate 'the lives, customs and discipline' set by 'Father Columba and his successors'.

Columcille

On some island I long to be,
a rocky promontory, looking on
the coiling surface of the sea.

To see the waves, crest on crest
of the great shining ocean, composing
a hymn to the creator, without rest.

To see without sadness the strand
lined with bright shells, and birds
lamenting overhead, a lonely sound.

To hear the whisper of small waves
against the rocks, that endless sea-
sound, like keening over graves.

To watch the sea-birds sailing
in flocks, and most marvellous
of monsters, the turning whale.

To see the shift from ebbtide
to flood and tell my secret name:
'He who set his back on Ireland.'

Version: John Montague
from *The Faber Book of Irish Verse*

Columcille in Exile

My heart is broken in two for love of my beautiful land. If death should suddenly take me, the cause is grief for my home.

If all Alba were mine, from its centre out to its coast, I would gladly exchange it for a field in a valley of Durrow or Derry.

Carry westwards my blessing, to Eire carry my love. Yet carry also my blessing east to the shores of Alba.

DOGMAEL   14 June

In Brittany, this fifth-century Welsh monk was invoked to help children learn to walk, in Wales he is particularly remembered in Pembrokeshire, where the ruins of a twelfth-century Benedictine abbey dedicated to him stand above the Teifi Estuary across the water from Cardigan. In the church that stands in the ruins of this abbey, you will find an inscribed ogham stone, probably dating from Dogmael's time. It commemorates a Prince of North Wales, and was being used as a footbridge across a stream when it was discovered in 1858.

TRILLO   15 June

At Llandrillo in the east of Gwynedd, an oratory carved with Irish designs stands over a baptismal spring dedicated to this fifth-century abbot. He is also remembered in another Llandrillo further to the west in old Merionethshire. The waters of that well were said to be a powerful cure for rheumatism.

JULIOT   16 June

Probably one of the daughters of Brychan (6 April), Juliot is remembered in the Cornish churches of St Juliot near Boscastle and Lanteglos near Camelford, which is also dedicated to her. She is thought to have been connected with the Celtic monastery on the cliffs of the Tintagel headland.

ISMAEL   16 June

Several dedications to Ismael (or Ishmael) are to be found in Dyfed, in the extreme south-west of Wales. One of them, a tiny church in a wood by the village of this name off the north coast of Milford Haven, was built on the site where the saint had his hermit's cell and around which his teaching monastery grew. The present church was built by Caradoc, a later Welsh saint of the twelfth century.

Ismael, who lived in the sixth century, was a disciple of David (1 March), Dyfrig (14 November) and Teilo (9 February). He was to succeed David as Bishop of Menevia.

NECTAN   17 June

A saint of the sixth century, Nectan was said to be the most important of the twenty-four holy children of Brychan, King of Powys (6 April), from whom Brecon gets its name. Like many other leaders of the Welsh Celtic church in his time, Nectan left his native country, possibly to escape the ravages of the yellow plague, and sailed south across the Bristol Channel. However, unlike many other missionary Welsh men and women, he did not set out alone or with one or two companions. A large group of people, variously described as relatives or followers went with Nectan over the water.

However, once they had made a landing on the rocky north Devon coast near Hartland Point, Nectan set out to live a solitary life as a forest hermit, and only met his fellow settlers on the last day of every year. His life, written in the twelfth century, tells us that one June day a gang of brigands attacked and murdered him in the course of stealing the cattle which Nectan had been given by a swineherd, whose pigs he had rescued. The story of his death is linked to the Celtic cult of the sacred severed head, for it is claimed that it was by beheading that he was killed, and that immediately after his head had been severed from his body he walked half a mile to a woodland spring. As he put the bleeding head in those waters they took on the strength, healing power and wisdom of the saint.

A great cult was made of Nectan in the early Middle Ages when his feast was kept with much ceremony at Launceston, Exeter and Wells. In the eleventh century, Bishop Lyfing of Crediton provided Nectan's church at Stoke by Hartland Point with a sculptured reliquary, and a century later the Augustinian canons of Hartland Abbey restored his shrine and cared for it until the Reformation.

There are five dedications to Nectan in Devon and Cornwall and many places along the coast between the two counties are associated with the saint. One of my favourites lies inland from the Valley of the Rocks to the east of Tintagel. Here in a wooded glen, unfortunately flanked by quarry workings, a magnificent waterfall rushes through a hole in the rocks high above the stream it feeds.

MOLING   17 June

Moling, a Leinster man of the seventh century, became a monk at Glendalough. Later he lived as a hermit by the River Barrow, where he fulfilled one of the traditional roles of a recluse, helping travellers by running a ferry service across the water. Later he became Bishop of Ferns to the north of Wexford.

As a follower of Kevin (3 June), he was naturally a lover of animals and many tales are told about his pet fox. According to one account, the fox ate one of the saint's hens, and tried to replace it by sneaking off to a convent and substituting one belonging to the nuns. Moling, who knew what had happened, reproved his pet, saying 'You have stolen again, take the hen back to the nuns and put her in a safe place, and try to live without stealing like other animals'.

The *Book of Mulling*, a ninth-century gospel book described by the twelfth-century Gerald of Wales, is probably a copy of one made by this saint. It survives in a jewelled shrine in the library of Trinity College, Dublin, and is valuable in that it contains a plan of Moling's monastery at Ferns.

GOVAN   20 June

Most visitors to the south coast of Pembrokeshire will have made a point of climbing down the cleft in the cliffs to the little chapel of St Govan's. The saint is said to have lived here as a hermit in the sixth century, and you can still see the tiny cell that he occupied in the seaward corner of the chapel, a place from which only a glimpse of the sky is possible.

In the church of St Gobán, to the west of Laon (a French town famous for the manufacture of glassware), the skull of an Irish hermit murdered on 20 June 670, is preserved in the parish church. He was thought to have been a contemporary of Fiacre (30 August) and to have been nicknamed Goban (little mouth) on account of his actual feature, or more likely because of his silent way of life. I feel that the two saints, although apparently divided by almost a century of time, are in fact the same person.

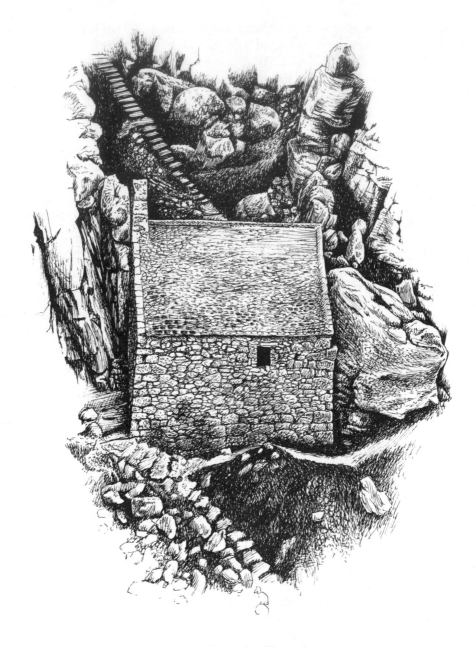

St Govan's Chapel

MEWAN 21 June

Born in South Wales, Mewan became a disciple of Samson
(28 July), and a companion of Austell (28 June) with whom
he journeyed through Cornwall on his way to Brittany. Once
there he founded a monastery in the Forest of Broceliande and
another where St Méen has now grown, which became a place
of pilgrimage for the whole of France.

GERMOE 24 June

A monk from Ireland, Germoe landed in Cornwall at the Hale
Estuary accompanied by Breaca (4 June). He crossed the peninsula
to settle in the place that bears his name between Helston and
Marazion. In a wall painting in the church in Breage he is shown
wearing a crown and sceptre, no doubt because he appears as a
monarch in one of the legends connected with Breaca. In the fifteenth century a little stone building comprising a triple seat under
a gable and two pointed arches was erected in the churchyard. John
Leland recorded it and described it as St Germoe's chair.

MOLUAG 25 June

Born in the north of Ireland in 530, an Irish Pict of the clan
Dalaraidhe, Moluag became a monk at Bangor, and from there
at the age of thirty-two he went to Scotland to found a monastery
on the island of Lismore. He arrived there a year before Columcille
(9 June) settled on Iona. Columcille is reported to have wanted to
make his own settlement on Lismore; instead he visited Moluag
there and preached under the great yew tree growing on the
high-tide island of Berrera at the western end of the island.
Moluag's own settlement in the north of Lismore was close to
a megalithic site surmounted by a high cairn which once marked
the funeral pyres of Pictish kings.

From Lismore, Moluag made missionary journeys to Skye and
the Outer Hebrides, where, in Lewis, his name was invoked for
centuries as a cure for madness. He also went to Raasay, where
there are some very ancient crosses showing how the Celtic wheel
developed from the ancient Christian Chi-Rho symbol, designed

from the Greek characters for Christ. He also went along the Great Glen to the east and founded settlements at Fort Augustus, Glen Urquhart on the shores of Loch Ness, and at Rosemarkie on the Black Isle, where Pictish symbols on a slab of sandstone are said to mark his grave. He died at Ardclach in Nairnshire on this day in 592.

His crozier, Bacchuill Mor, the great staff, a piece of blackthorn 34 inches (86 cm) long and originally covered in copper is preserved on Lismore in Bachuil village in the care of the Livingstones; having been for some time in the custody of the Dukes of Argyll.

AUSTELL   28 June

Disciple and companion of Mewan (21 June) in whose tomb at St Méen he is buried. The two friends are said to have founded neighbouring parishes in Cornwall, that of Austell being the best known because of the vast china clay industry in the area.

Milking Song

Come, Mary Virgin, to my cow,
Come, great Bride, the beauteous,
Come, thou milkmaid of Jesus Christ,
    And place thine arms beneath my cow.
        Ho my heifer, ho my gentle heifer.

Lovely black cow, pride of the shieling,★
First cow of the byre, choice mother of calves,
Wisps of straw round the cows of the townland,
    A shackle of silk on my heifer beloved.
        Ho my heifer, ho my gentle heifer.

My black cow, my black cow,
A like sorrow afflicts me and thee,
Thou grieving for thy lovely calf,
    I for my beloved son under the sea,
        My beloved only son under the sea.

Collected by Alexander Carmichael

★ Shieling: the place of the summer pasture

JUNE PILGRIMAGE

Columcille's Hermitage, Iona

Iona is always a special goal of pilgrimage, and naturally it is particularly good to be there on Columcille's day (June 9th). If you are able to manage that, then go into the wilder north-eastern part of the island, climbing the hill of Dun I, and then turning to the west. Here on the rough moor, you will find a low circular wall surrounding an area some 18 feet (5 m) in diameter. Although these stones are superficially less impressive than those marking a nearby cattle stell, probably dating from the eighteenth century, they outline the hermitage where Columcille went on his own to pray.

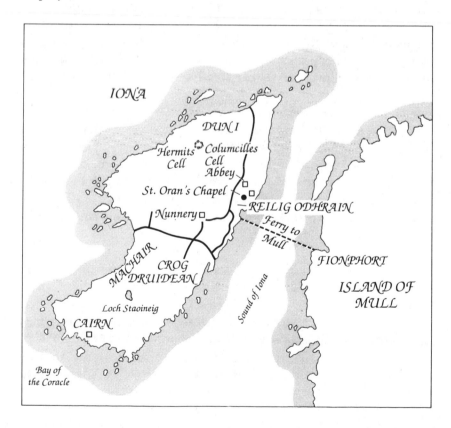

 # July

Wells and Springs

July, which is often a time of drought, is a good month in which to consider the essential part that water plays in our lives and perhaps to visit holy wells, which should remind us of the reverence that we should have for its source. Some people suggest that these wells were not declared sacred on account of the miraculous powers of their waters, but because a holy place would be safeguarded from pollution. Whether such an attitude should be deemed cynical or not, I do not know, but I am certain that the matter is still pertinent for us today, and that it would be a blessed thing if we were to treat our water supplies with the reverence that the followers of the Celtic saints gave to the wells associated with particular holy men.

The marvellous thing is that, in story after story, we are told how the wandering Celts made their settlements at places where oxen who were drawing their carts refused to move further; or, as in the case of Glastonbury, where a pig farrowed. Behind all these stories is the animal instinct for discovering a drinking hole, a water-finding sense more finely developed than that of the most sensitive water-diviner. It is, perhaps, the most important instance of our dependency on our fellow creatures.

From their druidic ancestors, the Christian Celts inherited a belief in the sanctity of the human head as the repository of the soul, and this belief also became linked to certain wells. Caitlín Matthews in her *The Elements of the Celtic Tradition* reminds us that in several Irish stories 'the taking of the head completes the sacrifice of the sacred king', and that when King Conaire's champion, MacCecht, having been sent to fetch water, returns to find his sovereign's head being cut off by his enemies, he immediately kills the murderers and pours water down the throat of the severed head. For which deed the severed head of Conaire finds powers of speech and declares 'He gives a drink, he saves a king, he doth a noble deed'. In much the same manner, we shall find that there are many traditional stories telling of Celtic saints, killed by beheading, whose deaths are linked to the gushing forth of fresh springs. Often a new well appears on the spot where the severed head falls to the ground, or in some cases, as in the stories of St Decuman (27 August) and St Nectan (17 June) in the West Country, at the places to which the murdered saint has carried his head. However, the best known of all such wells must be that of Winefride of Holywell in North Wales, whose healing waters still draw crowds of pilgrims.

Caitlín Matthews links this holy aspect of sacrificial beheading to the tradition of the Grail and one immediately thinks of the Chalice Well in Glastonbury. She cites the story of Bran the Blessed from the *Mabinogion*, for at his beheading he became a bridge to the other world; and certainly the Druids regarded wells as entrances to eternity, a belief which the Christians could understand in terms of those sacred sites where light and life break through the dark rock.

There is an unfounded, but potent, tradition that Patrick (17 March) was one of the saints who met his death by beheading, a belief that adds force to the healing powers of the wells associated with him. One such is the well of Maumeer in the Mamturk Mountains, a spring that still draws pilgrims and whose waters are said to have healing powers for both men and animals. Dr D.C.C. Pochin Mould assures us that this well is so powerful that the cure will begin as soon as the messenger sets out to fetch the water.

That a well should have such telepathic knowledge of intent is consistent with the Irish druidic notion of wells as the source of wisdom and not only of the great rivers that feed the land. Above the most powerful of these wells in the centre of Ireland, nine hazel trees grew. Their nuts which contained all wisdom fell into the water and were devoured by salmon, so that anyone eating of that fish was endowed with mystic inspiration. From that well, from which the seven chief rivers of Ireland took their source, all wells acquired a reputation for supernatural powers, which in the minds of the faithful followers of the saints were often represented by healing waters with specific properties for the cure of particular afflictions, the most common being madness and eye troubles. The association with eyes came about because wells were thought of as the eyes of the world, having sight of both time and eternity. The ability of some turbulent waters to cure madness is linked to the common belief in divine frenzy, the encounter with the forces of the other world that can lead to divinity or insanity, in the same way that spending a night on certain mountains, such as Cader Idris in north Wales, can turn the sleeper into a poet or a lunatic.

Whatever the disease, the healing power of the well water was usually only thought to be truly effective if the afflicted person slept after drinking or washing in the waters. In the case of St Fillan's pool in the west Highlands, the one to be cured of madness was left alone, bound tightly to a frame, by the stone font of the priory by the well. If the ropes that bound him were found to be slackened in the morning it was sign that he was cured, for he had been given strength to wrestle with the devil. In all cases, the sleep is an indication that all healing takes place in the depths of the unconscious rather than by conscious interference.

At the well of St Levan (14 October) in Cornwall, the eighteenth-century antiquarian, Dr Borlase, found a little chapel, 5 feet (1½ m) square and 7 feet (2 m) high. It was built on a platform above the saint's well, whose water, he said 'is reckoned very good for eyes, tooth-ache and the like, and when people have washed they are always advised to go into this chappell and sleep upon the stone which is the floor of it, for it must be remembered that whilst you are sleeping upon these consecrated stones the saint is sure to be dispensing his healing influence'.

People were also expected to sleep on a grassy mound called St Madron's Bed when they came to be healed at the well of that other Cornish saint. In coming to these waters they were following the example of John Trelil, a twenty-eight-year-old cripple, whose case was examined in 1641 by Joseph Hall, Bishop of Exeter. When John Trelil washed in the waters of this well as they ran through the nearby chapel, for centuries used as a baptistry, he only had to sleep for an hour and a half before he felt life returning to his damaged limbs. St Madron's Well is still a goal of pilgrimage, and services are still held in the chapel, although I do not think that many people sleep on this marshy ground. They do, however, leave prayer rags tied to the surrounding trees. These scraps of cloth keep their requests and intentions alive as they journey on, in much the same way as some of us light candles in church.

SERF 1 July

Thought to have been a disciple of the fifth-century Palladius (7 July), Serf had a monastery at Culross on the northern shore of the Firth of Forth. There he nurtured the infant Kentigern (13 January), educating him, in the words of the twelfth-century Jocelyn of Furness, 'like another Samuel, committed unto him and assigned by God'.

OUDACEUS 2 July

A nephew of Teilo (9 February) and the son of a princely Breton family who ruled 'over the whole land of Armorica', Oudaceus reversed the usual migratory journeys of the Celtic saints by coming north into Wales around 545. Until the middle of the sixteenth century he was particularly revered at Llandaff, and most of our knowledge of him comes from a twelfth-century life, which Canon G.H. Doble (*see* Bibliography) considered to be mainly an amalgam of holy legends. According to this account he was connected with a community at Llandogo on the banks of the Wye to the south of Monmouth. There he is said to have come into conflict with Gildas (29 January) who entered the forest to collect some timber for building.

GERMANUS OF MAN 3 July

Born in Brittany about 410, Germanus went to Ireland and worked with Patrick (17 March). At the age of thirty he came to South Wales and lived in the monastery founded by Illtyd (6 November). In 466 he was ordained Bishop of the Isle of Man.

The Protection of the Cattle

> Pastures smooth, long, and spreading,
> Grassy meads aneath your feet,
> The friendship of God the Son to bring you home
> To the field of the fountains,
>   Field of the fountains.

Closed be every pit to you,
Smoothed be every knoll to you,
Cosy every exposure to you.
Beside the cold mountains,
   Beside the cold mountains.

The care of Peter and of Paul,
The care of James and of John,
The care of Bride fair and of Mary Virgin,
To meet you and to tend you,
      Oh! the care of all the band
      To protect you and to strengthen you.

Collected by Alexander Carmichael

MORWENNA 5 July

An unusual version of the sacred head theme occurs in the story of
the sixth-century Morwenna, a descendant of Brychan (6 April).
When she came into Cornwall from Wales, she climbed up a cliff
carrying on her head a stone that she wanted to use to build her
church. The stone fell to the ground and where it struck a rock a
spring gushed forth. I think that this stone, like many others that
saints are reported to have carried with them, may well be taken
to represent the small portable altars that accompanied the saints
on their travels.

MONENNA 6 July

A holy well stands above the church at Killeavy, County Antrim,
where Monenna founded one of the most important Irish nun-
neries in the early years of the sixth century. Closely associated
with Brigid (1 February) and Patrick (17 March), she headed a
community of eight virgins and one widow. There is a record that
one of these women went to the college at Whithorn founded by
Ninian (26 August).

   Two churches stand end to end at Killeavy now, as they do
at Llantwit Major in Glamorgan. The one to the west contains
material from the eighth and ninth centuries and it has a Celtic
doorway with a massive granite lintel.

Morwenna

MAELRUAN   7 July

> On the nones of July the birds cease
> To sing the music of holidays
> For Maelruan from Tallaght.

These lines in the margin of the early ninth-century Martyrology of Tallaght in County Wicklow celebrate the founder of that monastery, who died in 792. One of the most influential members of the Culdee reform movement, whose name comes from *Céili Dé*, the servants of God, he kept his monks to a strict regime. They were vegetarian and allowed to drink nothing but water, and they were all advised to consult a soul friend (*anamachara*) at least once a year. Furthermore, in contrast to many of the wandering Celts, Maelruan was no advocate of restless travel and commanded his monks always 'to abide where thou art wont to be'.

Maelruan had a special reverence for St Michael whose feast was kept at Tallaght with great solemnity; and in the tradition of the Celtic church, he relied heavily on the Psalter. He drew particular strength from Psalm 118, the hymn of the Feast of Tabernacles, the Jewish harvest thanksgiving, which falls around Michaelmas.

BOISIL   7 July

In 651, the young Cuthbert (20 March) joined the community at Melrose where Boisil was prior. The original monastery stood by a bend in the Tweed a little to the east of the site chosen for the twelfth-century abbey. All that remains of the first settlement are a few scattered stones, one of which, carved with Celtic designs, serves as the lintel for an Edwardian summer-house. Boisil, described by Bede as 'a priest of great virtues and prophetic spirit', undertook many preaching journeys in the surrounding hills, a way of life that Cuthbert was to emulate. When Boisil was fatally struck down by the plague in 661, Cuthbert attended him, reading to him daily from the Gospel of St John.

PALLADIUS   7 July

There is some dispute as to whether the fifth-century Palladius is the same man as Germanus of Auxerre (31 July). However, as an apostle sent to Ireland to combat the Pelagian heresy, there seems to be more evidence for his separate existence than there is for Patrick's (17 March). According to some accounts, in the year before his death in 432, Pope Celestine sent him to become the first bishop of 'the Scots believing in Christ'. So he crossed the water from Ireland and founded a church at Fordun near Aberdeen, where he died.

URITH   8 July

According to a rhyming Latin poem, now in Trinity College, Cambridge, Urith, born in East Stowford, Devon, at an unspecified date, was killed at the instigation of her pagan stepmother by a group of haymakers, who struck her with their scythes. A stream sprang out of the ground from the place where she fell. She is remembered in the church at Chittlehampton, the building cost of whose tower is reputed to have been met out of the offerings left at her shrine. As Urith is a Celtic name, it is possible that the story of this little-known saint represents an account of the overthrow of Christian Devonian Celts by pagan Saxon invaders.

KILIAN   8 July

In 689, Kilian, an Irish monk from Mullagh, was martyred in Germany because he criticized the tribal king Gozbert for marrying his brother's widow. Kilian was one of the wandering Irish missionaries who ventured deeply into the Continent. He sailed up the River Main to Wurzeburg with eleven companions.

DROSTAN   11 July

A friend of Columcille (9 June), Drostan founded the monastery of Deer, in the heart of Pictland, now Aberdeenshire. The story is that the two friends came there together towards the end of the sixth century, and that the place was given its name from the Gaelic *deara* (tears) because they wept when it was time for the elderly Columcille to return to Iona and they knew that they would never meet again in this world.

DONALD   15 July

The father of nine daughters, Donald lived in the late seventh
century at Ogilvy (Forfarshire). On his wife's death he became
religious and took the girls to Meigle, a village that now stands on
the A94 to the north-east of Coupar Angus. There his daughters are
said to have danced in the oak woods of the Sidlaw Hills, hoping to
produce visions of their future husbands. Perhaps the girls were
inspired to follow that ancient pagan practice by the carving of
the Celtic horned god, Cernunnos, engraved among Christian
symbols on the elaborately decorated Pictish stones which you
can still see at Meigle.

The lilies with their silver leaves
Border the streamlets in the meadows;

God gave them their fair clothing,
Their sweet scent that is wafted far over the land.

From *The Land of Pardons* by Anatole le Braz, translated by
Frances M. Gostling (Methuen, 1906)

Nunc Viridant Segetes

The standing corn is green, the wild in flower,
     The vines are swelling, 'tis the sweet o' the year,
Bright-winged the birds, and heavens shrill with song,
     And laughing sea and earth and every star.

Sedulius Scottus, ninth-century, translated by Helen Waddell

CONAN   23 July

The church at Washaway (Cornwall) is dedicated to Conan, an
obscure saint thought to have been a companion of Petroc
(4 June). It is in this Egloshayle (the church by the estuary),
at the place where Conan probably landed, that his feast is
celebrated.

DECLAN 24 July

Early in the fifth century, before Patrick (17 March) began his mission to Ireland, Declan founded the church at Ardmore on the headland by Youghal harbour. The ruins of his settlement and the round tower beside them still stand on the sandy beach. The story goes that the standing stones at the Dog's Pass in the Comeragh Mountains mark the place where Declan was offered dog meat disguised as mutton by the pagan tribal leader, Dercan. The saint was not deceived, but restored the dog to life and sent it flying across the hill. In old age, Declan is supposed to have visited Ailbe (12 September) in Rome.

Milking

Bless, O God, my little cow,
    Bless, O God, my desire;
Bless Thou my partnership
    And the milking of my hands, O God.

Bless, O God, each teat,
    Bless, O God, each finger;
Bless Thou each drop
    That goes into my pitcher, O God!

Collected by Alexander Carmichael

SAMSON 28 July

At the beginning of the sixth century, the child Samson was taken to Illtyd (6 November) to be educated by him at his monastery of Llantwit Major on the Glamorgan coast. It was from there that he went for ordination as deacon and priest and set out to become one of the most revered of the Welsh travelling missionaries. We have two somewhat conflicting accounts of his life. The more reliable one was written in the seventh century; the other appears in a twelfth-century life of Illtyd and was obviously written for the glorification of the monastery at Llantwit Major.

According to the earlier biography, Samson left Illtyd while he was still a young man and established his own monastery on Ynys Pyr (Caldey Island). While he was there he was visited by some

'distinguished Irishmen' returning from a pilgrimage to Rome.
Samson went to Ireland with them, and while he was there he
obtained an Irish 'chariot', some sort of horse-drawn cart, in
which he could carry his books on his travels. He took this cart
back to Caldey, a two-day voyage from the Howth Peninsula of
Dublin, and it accompanied him wherever he went. He did not
remain long on Caldey, but set out across the Bristol Channel
to land at St Kew, near Padstow. There he stayed and planned a
journey that would enable him to visit many places in Cornwall
before sailing for Brittany from Golant. We have one story of his
encounter with the pagan people of Cornwall, who revered the
ancient standing stones of the moor, ritual monuments of Bronze
Age peoples, and there before the Celts came north. With an iron
instrument, Samson carved the sign of the cross on the granite
(a near-miraculous feat in itself) and so hallowed for Christ the
prehistoric monument.

   The twelfth-century manuscript gives an altogether more florid
account of Samson's elevation to a Breton bishopric. We are told
that Samson heard that he had been elected Bishop of Dol, while
he was still with Illtyd at Llantwit Major. He was said to be so

distressed at the thought of leaving his beloved master that he wept bitterly, his tears falling into a stream 'that still bears his name'. This is thought to have been on the site of the old town well to the north-east of the church. Having made a solemn vow that after his death his body should be brought back to Wales and buried beside his master, he went with Illtyd to Llandaff. There Dyfrig (14 November) ordained him as deacon. While that ceremony was taking place both the two elders saw a a white dove perched on the young man's shoulder.

This account goes on to tell us that after Samson's death at Dol in 565, his body was put in a sarcophagus, which 'a mighty wind wafted lightly across the sea, like a wild fowl in flight, till it came down and landed safely like a ferry boat at the gate of Illtut [Illtyd]'.

Dol itself honoured Samson with a stained glass window made in the thirteenth century. It shows the Welsh saint on his travels with two companions. The boat is under full sail and captained by a cherub.

LUPUS OF TROYES   29 July

Born late in the fourth century, Lupus became a monk on the island of Lérins in the Mediterranean, and in 426 was ordained Bishop of Troyes. Three years later, he accompanied Germanus of Auxerre (31 July) to Britain. On his return to Gaul he was captured by Attila the Hun, and remained a hostage until Attila's defeat, whereupon he settled in the mountains as a hermit. He died in 478.

CROHAUN   30 July

A contemporary of Patrick (17 March), Crohaun had his hermitage in the mountains of Kerry. Two wells are said to have served his needs. The one at Kilcrohane is the goal of an annual pilgrimage on this date; and another charted by Dr D.D.C. Pochin Mould in her *Mountains of Ireland* (Gill & Macmillan, 1976) is at Windy Gap Pass on the ridge between Kilcrohane and Waterville. Dr Mould has identified the remains of the saint's cave on the mountain side, where copper ore was once mined. It was, here, in a quarry hole left by prehistoric workings that, she claims, Crohaun settled, a place marked by a vein of white quartzite.

NEOT   31 July

A ninth-century monk of Glastonbury, Neot became a hermit
on the south side of Bodmin Moor, settling near the shrine of
Gueryr (4 April) at the place that is now called after the later,
better-known saint. Neot's well, which stands a little apart from
the late fifteenth-century church which is dedicated to him, was
supposed to have supplied him with an endless supply of fish, in
gratitude for which he would daily stand in its waters reciting
the Psalter. The twelfth-century account of his life tells us that
three fish constantly swam in this well although the saint ate one
each day, and that this went on until Neot fell sick and could eat
nothing at all. His alarmed companions, hoping to tempt him
to sustenance, caught all three fish and cooked them in different
ways. This restored the saint to health in an unexpected way, for
Neot was so aghast at what had happened that he leapt up and
threw all three dishes into the well. Immediately three fish
swam away.

A hundred years after Neot's death in 877, his relics were taken
from Cornwall to grace the monastery founded by the Saxon
Leofric at Eynesbury, near St Ives, Cambridgeshire.

GERMANUS OF AUXERRE   31 July

Born of Romano-Gallician parents, Germanus was sent twice to
Britain to refute the Pelagian heresy (see pages 95–6). On his first
visit, having miraculously restored the sight of a ten-year-old girl,
he refuted the followers of Pelagius at the tomb of St Alban.
He then turned west and directed the Celtic forces against the
combined might of the Picts and Saxons. He defeated the pagans
by causing the British men to shout out 'Alleluia' three times
with such strength that the echo of their voices was irresistibly
terrifying to the attackers, who fled without a drop of blood
being shed.

Some years later, after Germanus had returned to the Continent,
there was a revival of the Pelagian heresy, and in 483 he returned
to Britain. Once more a miracle of healing ensured the defeat of
the heresy. In this case it was the crippled son of a local chieftain
who was healed by the apostle of Rome.

Despite his opposition to the teaching of the Celtic Pelagius,
Germanus clearly had a great affection for the people of the Celtic

church. He died in Ravenna in 448 while pleading the cause of the rebellious Bretons.

JULY PILGRIMAGE

Declan's Settlement, Ardmore

Before Patrick came to Ireland, Declan sailed west from Wales to found a Christian settlement on the Waterford coast to the east of Cork. According to the hagiographies, he built a cell and oratory on an island there, but finding it too small for his purpose he prayed for the sea to retreat, and spread his settlement over the resulting headland. The stone on which he is said to have made the crossing from Wales still lies on the beach and is reputed to have the power of curing rheumatism.

Apart from that holy ballast there are two other important relics here;
a 97 foot high, twelfth-century round tower with tapering walls, said
to be one of the finest in Ireland; and St Declan's house. The latter is
a steeply gabled building, claimed as the saint's oratory but probably
of a later date. In its south-east corner there is a grave trough where
they say Declan's body lay. There are two ogham-inscribed stones in
the nearby eleventh-century cathedral.

Lammas

The Season of Harvests

 # Luke

The gentle, four-winged, haloed calf adorned with triangles of red dots, the symbol for Luke in the *Book of Kells*, has something to tell us about the hidden strength and elegance of the evangelist whose feast is kept on 18 October. That is the time when nearly all the harvests are completed, and the great orange harvest moon heralds the close of the Celtic year. This flying creature – the cow that jumped over the moon – is going to take us from one mode of being to another. We are about to enter the next ring of a spiral.

Knowledgeable in Jewish lore and customs, Luke was a Gentile, writing for Gentiles in the finest Greek. His gospel, based largely on the work of Mark, and probably contemporary with that of Matthew, was written sometime after the destruction of the Temple in 70 CE.

Both Matthew and Luke drew on an unknown source or sources. Scholars label this Q, and use Q to explain sections of these gospels which do not appear in Mark. The notion of Q can embrace a number of written texts as well as oral traditions based on the words of Jesus. Although they have been lost to us, the texts and traditions may well have been familiar to the early Coptic church in Egypt, and so have come to Ireland with traders and travellers from North Africa.

Luke himself is almost as mysterious as Q. He dedicates both his gospel and Acts (his account of the early church) to a patron, Theophilus, whose name means lover of God. Theophilus was possibly a highly placed government official in the Roman empire; certainly, like Luke, he was a Gentile. Both of them must have been among those attracted to the Jewish tradition, adopting many of the customs of the synagogue, and probably at this time of year celebrating the harvest thanksgiving festival of Tabernacles. Knowing of the Jewish faith in the Messiah, Theophilus would have been a ready recipient of the good news which Luke had to relate.

Beyond these historical considerations, there are two aspects of

Luke's work that must have a particular appeal to the Celtic church. There is, first, the popular tradition that he was a physician. This may have no basis in fact, but it grew out of the emphasis that Luke gave to the poor and to despised outcasts in his gospel stories. Luke's concern is with humble people in all the struggles of their daily lives, in sickness and health. In that aspect of his work, he is as earthed as the ritual prayers and hymns of the Celtic church, which relate always to the recurring essentials of our material being.

At the same time, it is in Luke's gospel, and in Acts, that we learn most fully of the power of the Holy Spirit. This leads us both into the deep mystery of the Trinity, and defines and clarifies the thin veil which, in the Celtic vision, separates the world of time and matter from that of eternity and spirit.

 # August

Harvests

The season of Lammas begins on 1 August, the time of the druidic festival of Lughnasadh, held in honour of the great god Lug, who is commemorated in the Roman name for Carlisle, Luguvalium – the fortress of Lug. In the late twelfth century, Giraldus Cambrensis, then Archdeacon of Brecon, described a strangely mutated, Christian version of this festival, which took the form of a frenzied circle dance round the churchyard on the feast of the local saint, Almedha, which fell on 1 August. At that time, the men and girls, who came together from considerable distances, sang as they danced, 'then on a sudden falling on the ground in a fit, then jumping up in a frenzy, and representing with their hands and feet before the people whatever work they have unlawfully done on feast days'. So some mimed ploughing with oxen, others went through the motions of cobbling, tanning, spinning and weaving. All occupations concerned with the essential work of the fields and the welfare of the community, but all of which should be assigned to appropriate times and seasons.

Although the connections between the Almedha dance and the Lughnasadh are not easy to trace, it is clear that the former grew out of some ceremony designed to ensure that the corn should be safely gathered in. Then, as now, so much of the success of a harvest, dependent as it is on the vagaries of the weather, was out of human hands. People could only turn to God and their own good sense.

As the harvest came to its conclusion, before the corn was stored, probably in underground storage pits, the druidic worshippers of Lug had to take thought for the following year's harvest and reserve a supply of seed corn, which in itself became in part an offering to the gods of the harvest. In later years this offering was symbolized in many places by the elaborate corn dollies formed out of the last sheaf to be cut. Lammas is an Anglo-Saxon word

derived from hlaef-mas, the Mass Loaf. It was the custom for this
to be made from the first flour ground after the harvest.

In the Celtic Christian tradition, the reaping of the corn was as
much a matter for blessing as any other activity of the farming
year. In the reaping song below, particular attention is given to
the sickle, used to cut the corn, a reminder of the sanctity of the
tools we use.

> God, bless Thou Thyself my reaping,
> Each ridge, and plain, and field,
> Each sickle curved, shapely, hard,
> Each ear and handful in the sheaf,
> Each ear and handful in the sheaf.

In all their dealings with nature, and especially in those aspects of
nature that serve human purpose, the Druids and their Christian
successors were aware of the awe and respect in which we should
hold the material universe of God's creation, and the tools with
which we fashion it. In contrast to this, Wendell Berry reminds
us 'The so-called materialism of our own time is . . . at once
indifferent to spiritual concerns and insatiably destructive of the
material world'.

When the corn is gathered in, it is time for the harvest of the
hedges and orchards: the blackberries and the sacred apples –
which when cut in half horizontally reveal the perfect mandala
at the centre. Finally the harvest concludes with collecting and
storing the nuts; and we have to remember that to the Celts the
hazel nuts, particularly when the trees that bore them grew by a
spring, represented kernels of wisdom.

By Samhain, 1 November, all these fruits had to be gathered, for
anything left on the trees after that date would be contaminated by
evil. We still say of the tasteless blackberries of late September that
the devil has spat on them.

So the Celtic year ends, as our Christian year still does, with
a thanksgiving for the harvests. In the Jewish tradition this
event is marked by the eight-day feast of Ingathering, more
generally known as Tabernacles. It is carried out in accordance
with Yahweh's instruction to Moses as recorded in Leviticus
that a feast should take place when the produce of the land
was harvested. The Jews were commanded to make booths or
rough shelters for themselves at this time, fashioned out of 'palm
branches, boughs of leafy trees and willows from the river bank'
and to dwell in them for the octet of the festival in memory of the

wanderings of the Exodus. By this means it would be made clear that there is no abiding place in this world, a sentiment dear to the hearts of the wandering Celts. As a further reminder of God's guidance through the desert, great candles were lit at this time in the temple in Jerusalem. In northern latitudes, the end of harvest coincides with the coming of the shorter days, the start of the dark months. So a new cycle begins.

CENYDD   1 August

A hermit who lived for some time on the high-tide island of Burry Holms off the coast of the Gower Peninsula in South Wales, Cenydd is another saint whose birth became the subject of the folklore motif of the young child cast out for almost certain death. In this case, the baby was said to be the son of an incestuous union, born deformed as a mark of his parent's depravity, one leg being bent double with the calf attached to the thigh. Such an obvious penalty for the shame of his conception caused his father, a Welsh prince, to put the baby in a coracle made of reeds and push it out to sea. The child was miraculously saved by seagulls who took him gently out of his frail craft and carried him to a ledge of rock on Gower. There they made a nest of feathers for him. Nine days later an angel appeared carrying a bell from which the baby could suckle. Some versions of the story tell us that the milk came from heaven, others that a doe walked out of the forest to the cliff edge each day and spurted her milk into the bell.

Another more sober Welsh version of Cenydd's life makes him the son of Gildas (29 January), but whatever the real truth of his origin, this Welsh monk finally went to Brittany and settled at Ploumelin.

ALMEDHA   1 August

Said to be a daughter, but more probably a grand-daughter, of Brychan (6 April), Almedha was killed on a hill near Brecon by heathen Saxons in the sixth century. A chapel was put up at the place where she died, about a mile (1½ km) to the east of the town. Although roofless, it was still standing in in the twelfth century when Giraldus wrote of the festival dance described in this month's introduction (page 195). A well now marks the site.

SIDWELL 2 August

William of Worcester and John Leland both mention a healing
well in Exeter dedicated to Sidwell who, according to a late
medieval catalogue of English saints, was killed there when her
pagan stepmother incited the reapers in the harvest fields to cut
off her head. This story makes her into a sort of corn goddess
dying for the fertility of the land, but it is also very similar to
to the account given of her sister Juthwara (28 November). In
neither case do we have any idea of the date when the murders
were supposed to have taken place.

Sidwell, whose name is surely made up of the scythe and the well
with which she is associated, is portrayed with these emblems in
the stained glass of Exeter Cathedral and in the carvings of several
Devon rood screens.

Reaping

God, bless Thou Thyself my reaping,
Each ridge, and plain, and field,
Each sickle curved, shapely, hard,
Each ear and handful in the sheaf,
     Each ear and handful in the sheaf.

Bless each maiden and youth,
Each woman and tender youngling,
Safeguard them beneath Thy shield of strength,
And guard them in the house of the saints,
     Guard them in the house of the saints.

Encompass each goat, sheep and lamb,
Each cow and horse, and store,
Surround Thou the flocks and herds,
And tend them to a kindly fold,
     Tend them to a kindly fold.

For the sake of Michael head of hosts,
Of Mary fair-skinned branch of grace,
Of Bride smooth-white of ringleted locks,
Of Columba of the graves and tombs,
     Columba of the graves and tombs.

Collected by Alexander Carmichael

SITHNEY 4 August

William of Worcester claimed to have seen Sithney's tomb at the place of that name near Helston in Cornwall, where sick and mad dogs were taken to drink from the healing well. The story goes that Sithney was so alarmed at being appointed to be the patron of girls, whom he felt sure would be for ever pestering him for rich husbands and fine clothes, that he claimed he would far rather look after mad dogs.

MOLUA 4 August

A disciple of Finnian of Clonard (12 December) while he was still a boy, Molua went on to Bangor to be taught by Comgall (11 May), where he became a monk. There he so distinguished himself both by his piety and his scholarship that Comgall encouraged him to set up his own settlement. With a few companions he set out first of all for Mount Luachra in Limerick; and from there he went on to establish his own monastery, Killaloe in County Clare.

There he devised a rule, read and approved by Pope Gregory the Great, and many monks came to join him. Although his discipline was strict, he appears to have handled his community with a certain wry humour. To one monk who wanted to have the fire all to himself he demonstrated that the heat was sufficient for at least two people by firmly settling himself beside the selfish brother; and he cut down thistles alongside another who objected to manual work. In 1929, the area of Molua's monastery was submerged by the hydro-electric works on the Shannon.

Having consulted his bishop about his successor, and appointed his principal disciple Flannan (18 December), Molua died in 605.

OSWALD 5 August

For seventeen years, Oswald, an Anglian prince of the royal house of Northumbria, lived in exile on Iona, while his maternal uncle, Edwin, ruled his country. On Edwin's death, he came back to his country with his older brother Eanfrid, and when the latter was killed by the Celtic Cadwallan, an ally of the pagan Penda of Mercia, Oswald became king. In 634, he defeated Cadwallan near Hadrian's Wall, at a place that became known as Heavenfield. A

Oswald

large wooden cross stands by the roadside there now, on the spot where Oswald is said to have set up one such before the battle, assembling his people there to pray for victory, and saying 'Let us all kneel and jointly beseech the true and living God Almighty, in his mercy, to defend us from the haughty and fierce enemy; for he knows that we have undertaken a just war for the safety of our nation'.

On the night before the battle, Oswald, we are told, had a dream in which Columcille (9 June) appeared to him in angelic splendour and promised him victory. As soon as peace was restored and Oswald had established his government, he sent to Iona for a young man to bring the Christianity he had learnt there to his people.

The first to arrive, a monk named Corman, was too strict to appeal to the mixed races of Northumbria, so in his place Aidan (31 August) came to establish the monastery of Lindisfarne. He and Oswald worked closely together, Oswald acting as interpreter for the Gaelic-speaking monk; and as Bede says, it must have been 'a touching spectacle to see the king, who had, during his long exile, thoroughly learnt the Celtic tongue, translating to the great chiefs and the principal officials of his court, the lords and thanes, the sermons of the bishop, who, as yet, spoke but imperfectly the language of the Anglo-Saxons'.

Oswald was only to live to the age of thirty-eight. He was killed at Masefield in Shropshire in a battle against the forces of Penda, bent on revenging Cadwallan's death. He died with the words 'My God, save their souls' on his lips, as he thought of his Northumbrian people. His body was dismembered, his head and hands being set up on stakes to intimidate the conquered nation. A year later his brother Oswy retrieved them, taking the head back to Lindisfarne and leaving the hands in the royal chapel at Bamburgh Castle.

LIDE 8 August

The Scilly island now known as St Helen's was once the chosen hermitage of Lide or Elid, a saint of unknown date. Remains of a hut and a tomb that is thought to be his have been found there; and a community under the rule of Tavistock Abbey flourished on the island in the Middle Ages. At that time a seven-year indulgence was granted to anybody who visited that shrine on this day – Lide's festival, at Christmas, or on Midsummer Day – the Feast of John the Baptist.

BETTELIN 10 August

A hermit who has a shrine and a well dedicated to him at Stafford, Bettelin was said to be the son of a Mercian prince who went to Ireland and married an Irish princess. He brought her back to England for the birth of their child, an event that was to cost her life, for while Bettelin went to find the midwife, wolves made their way into the royal palace and devoured both mother and child. Overcome with grief, Bettelin, whose date is unknown, spent the rest of his life as a hermit.

BLANE 11 August

A nephew of the sixth-century Cathan, who founded the monastery of Kingarth on the Isle of Bute, Blane spent seven years in Ireland as a disciple of Comgall (11 May) and Kenneth (11 October) At the end of that time he returned to his native Bute, making the crossing, it is said, with his mother, in a boat with neither oars nor rudder. Having been welcomed back by Cathan, who nominated him as his successor at Kingarth, Blane journeyed to Rome to receive the Pope's blessing.

Two miracles are attributed to him. One has him making fire from his finger ends; the other, of more importance, has him restoring the body of a blind boy to life, giving him back his sight and cleansing him from his sins.

Blane later founded a monastery on the mainland to the north of Stirling near the site where Dunblane Cathedral stands by the river. A bell, reputed to be his, is preserved there; and the cathedral also contains a block of red sandstone thought to be the remnants of his preaching cross. Blane's settlement was to the east of the present cathedral site, a cluster of beehive huts on a hilltop inside the walls of an old Pictish fort which defended the main route to the north.

MURTAGH 12 August

There are conflicting opinions as to whether Murtagh was converted by Patrick (17 March) or was a contemporary of Columcille
(9 June). The second alternative seems to be the most likely. In
any case he was undoubtedly connected with the monastery on
the island of Inishmurray in Donegal Bay. There you can see
the remains of the oratories and the beehive huts occupied by his
monks and their successors.

FACHANAN 14 August

A sixth-century Irish abbot, Fachanan founded the monastery of
Ross Carbery in West Cork. As a young man he was a disciple
of Ita (15 January) and he possibly also studied under Finbar (25
September). He is reported to have had his sight miraculously
restored after an attack of blindness.

Rising

Thou King of moon and sun,
　　Thou King of stars beloved,
Thou Thyself knowest our need,
　　O Thou merciful God of life.

Each day that we move,
　　Each time that we awaken,
Causing vexation and gloom
　　To the King of hosts Who loved us.

Be with us through each day,
　　Be with us through each night;
Be with us each night and day,
　　Be with us each day and night.

Collected by Alexander Carmichael

ARMEL 16 August

Reputed to have been born in South Wales, a cousin of Samson (28 July) and Cadfan (1 November), Armel went to Brittany on becoming a monk. There he founded at least two monasteries. In the fifteenth century, Henry VII, who believed that he had been saved from shipwreck off the Breton coast by Armel's intercession, encouraged his cult. You can see a statue of this saint in Henry VII's chapel in Westminster Abbey, another representation on Cardinal Morton's tomb in Canterbury Cathedral, a figure of the saint on a painted reredos in Romsey Abbey, and an alabaster figure in Stonyhurst College.

Armel is usually represented in armour, leading a dragon by a stole tied round its neck. The legend is that he took the creature to Mount St Armel and ordered it to leap into the river below. Followers of his cult believed that he had the power to intercede for many diseases including headache, fever, gout and colic.

HELEN 18 August

The twelfth-century historian, Geoffrey of Monmouth, claimed that Helen, mother of the Emperor Constantine and discoverer of the relic of the true Cross, was a British woman, daughter of King Ceol of Colchester. In the Welsh *Mabinogion*, she is described as a Welsh princess, bride of the self-styled emperor, Magnus Maximus, who was led by a dream to find her. This tradition was strong enough for the belief to grow up that she was responsible for the Roman roads (now marked on Ordnance Survey maps as the Sarn Helen) which link Wales from north to south. (*See also* Helen of Caernarvon, 22 May.)

MOCHETUS 19 August

Mochetus, who died in 535, was the son of an Irish bard called Hoa. The legends that grew up around him include the story that an angel taught him to write, and that he later showed the slate bearing the heavenly alphabet to the Pope. He is not to be confused with the fifth-century abbot of the same name, who with twelve companions helped Patrick (17 March) in the conversion of Ireland, and whose feast is also celebrated on this day.

OSWIN   20 August

A nephew of Oswald (5 August), Oswin succeeded to the throne
of the northern part of Northumbria in 642, and like his uncle
worked closely with Aidan (31 August). He assisted the bishop
on his missionary journeys, and even managed to persuade the
prelate, who preferred to journey on foot so that he might talk
to the people he met along the way, to take the gift of a horse so
that at least he could cross the rivers dry shod.

Aidan accepted the King's best steed, but he had not ridden far
when he met a beggar and immediately leapt to the ground and
gave the reins to the poor man, making him a gift of the horse.
When Oswin asked Aidan why he had done such a foolish thing,
Aidan replied 'O King, the horse which is the son of a mare, is
surely less precious than the man who is the son of God'. These
words apparently convinced the King of the need for humility and
generosity at all times.

Oswin was not destined to reign for long. On 20 August 651
he fell in battle against his uncle Oswy, who wanted to control
the whole kingdom of Northumbria. By the end of the month,
Aidan too had died.

Bede tells us the Oswin was 'a man of handsome appearance
and great stature, pleasant in speech and courteous in manner.
He was generous to high and low alike and soon won the
affection of all by his kingly qualities of mind and body, so
that men of very high birth came from nearly every province
to his service.'

Oswin was buried at Tynemouth; and Oswy, in order to assuage
his guilt at having caused the death of such a beloved monarch,
built a monastery at the place where he fell.

ARNULF   22 August

Arnulf was a hermit who lived and died at Eynesbury (Cambridgeshire) before the relics of Neot (31 July) were transferred there from
Cornwall in the tenth century. The original name of the place
derives from Arnulf, although he was venerated there before the
Danes came to give their version, Eanulfesbyrig, to denote the
saint's settlement.

TYDFIL   23 August

One of the daughters of Brychan (6 April), Tydfil, said to have been murdered by pagan Saxons, was buried to the south of the Brecon Beacons, and so gave her name to Merthyr Tydfil (the place of the martyrdom of Tydfil).

GENESIUS OF ARLES   25 August

Despite his Roman name, Genesius or Genny, who was martyred at the beginning of the twelfth century, was a Celt. During the persecutions instigated by the Emperor Diocletius, he was a government clerk, and it was because he refused to write out edicts of persecution against Christians that he met his death. He was beheaded on the banks of the Rhone.

EBBA   25 August

Sister of Oswald (5 August) and Oswy, joint Kings of Northumbria, Ebba founded and ruled the double monastery of Coldingham, situated on St Abb's Head, subsequently named after her. It is said that this 500 feet (150 m) high headland was chosen for the site because when Ebba had already been consecrated as a nun by Aidan (31 August); the King of Scots, desirous of marrying her, pursued her towards the coast. Taking refuge on the headland, she bade the sea fill the valley between it and the Lammermuir Range inland, so checking the King's advance.

For thirty years Ebba ruled her double monastery, in complete ignorance, so her biographers say, of the lack of discipline there. She was finally enlightened when one of the priests attached to the community told her that when he visited the cells he found 'All, all the men and all the women either fast asleep, or waking to mischief. Instead of praying and reading in their cells, they are organising little picnics in the them, with food and drink, or assembling for tittle-tattle.' The same priest prophesied that the monastery would be destroyed for its evil ways and indeed soon after Ebba died in 683 it was burnt down.

NINIAN   26 August

According to his biographers, Ninian was a very tall man physically, as well as being a giant of the Celtic church. Because of
his stature and general physique, his father, a Galloway chieftain,
wanted him to become a soldier; but from an early age, Ninian
was determined to dedicate his life to God.

He was born on the northern shores of the Solway Firth, in the
middle of the fourth century, and the place was to become a focus
of his work. For it was here in 397 that he founded the monastic
college of Whithorn, and built the first stone church in Britain. It
was known as Candida Casa, the White House; and in Gaelic it was
often referred to as Taigh Martin, because Ninian dedicated it to
his teacher, Martin of Tours (11 November), whom he visited on
his return from a journey to Rome. Martin died in the year that
the Candida Casa was completed.

In the mid twelfth century, one of the thirty-five houses of the
French Premonstratensian order to be set up in Britain was settled
on the same site; and it was not until excavations in 1949 that the
fourth-century church was revealed. The building was almost

The medieval priory church at Whithorn

square, measuring 15 by 14 feet (4½×4m), and it was constructed, according to Daphne D.C Pochin Mould's description in *Scotland of the Saints* (Batsford, 1952), 'of local rocks, slates and shales set in greenish clay'. Walls over 3 feet (1 m) thick, were still covered in some white mortar, and the whole bore a strong resemblance to the Celtic church that had been discovered on the cliffs at Tintagel.

Our knowledge of Ninian's life comes partly from an eighth-century poem, and partly from a hagiography composed by the twelfth-century monk, Ailred of Rievaulx, who was living in Scotland at the time of its composition. His work was no doubt stimulated and encouraged, if not commissioned, by Queen Margaret who was seeking to obtain the sanction of ancient traditions in an attempt to keep the Scottish church outside the orbit of Rome.

It is from these lives that we learn of Ninian's long journey across the Alps to Rome, and of his visit to Martin of Tours on the way home. If indeed he did visit Martin at Marmoutier, he would have realized how his teacher spent long days in solitude in a cave in the cliffs of the surrounding mountains; for when Ninian returned to his native Galloway, he made himself such a hermitage, a few miles away from his monastery. He chose a narrow cave, no more than a fissure in the Silurian rock, by the shore of the Solway Firth. From here he could look south to the Isle of Man, sacred in druidic lore to the sea god, and later dedicated to the archangel Michael; while to the west he might look across to the Rhins of Galloway, and the early Christian settlement of Kirkmadrine, from which as a boy he might well have had his first intimations of Christianity.

Ninian's cave was for centuries the goal of pilgrimage, and the rough crosses cut into the rock bear witness to the medieval travellers who came here. Long before their day, Whithorn flourished as one of the main colleges of the Celtic church, and also as a base from which missions went out to the Picts.

The numerous Ninian dedications throughout Scotland, extending as far as Orkney and Shetland, probably do not always represent Ninian's actual presence there, but a mission undertaken by one of his disciples. However it is probably safe to trust Bede's account that 'The southern Picts, who live on this side of the mountains [the Grampians], are said to have abandoned the errors of idolatry . . . and accepted the true Faith through the preaching of Bishop Ninian, a most reverend and holy man of British race'.

Robert Van de Weyer in *Celtic Fire*, an anthology of Celtic Christian literature, included a catechism supposedly devised by Ninian, which claimed that the fruit of study was 'To perceive the eternal word of God reflected in every plant and insect, every bird and animal, and every man and woman'.

DECUMAN   27 August

Born of noble parents in South Wales during the seventh century, Decuman sailed across the Bristol Channel, landing at Watchet. The medieval life tells us that he made that crossing on a bundle of rushes and that he took his cow with him. Once he arrived on the Somerset coast, he made himself a hermitage and lived in a hut of wattles, which he erected in a small forest clearing. For sustenance he had the milk from his cow.

Perhaps it was desire for the cow that caused a robber to attack him. It happened while Decuman was at prayer, and his assailant struck off his head. The familiar story follows. Decuman carried his head down to his well, and there he washed it, so sanctifying the waters. A somewhat far-fetched coda to this particular version of the severed head and the sacred spring has Decuman swimming back to Wales with his head under his arm.

The story of Decuman's life was reconstructed in the Middle Ages by a Canon of Wells Cathedral where his cult was fostered – as it was at Muchelney Abbey near Langport, where the monks regarded this day as the principal festival in the calendar.

Decuman, whose name means collector of tithes, was probably a Roman Briton. H. M. Porter, author of *The Celtic Church in Somerset*, argues that this is born out by the Roman-inscribed stone in the parish church of Cwm Du in the Rhiangoll Valley to the north of Crickhowell, where there was once a chapel dedicated to Decuman.

At Watchet, the church which Coleridge envisaged as the Ancient Mariner's final landfall, naturally carries a dedication to Decuman. The well lies beside a path going downhill from the churchyard. Its waters gush out of a spring and then fall into three terraced basins.

FIACRE 30 August

A patron of gardeners, and so always depicted with a spade, Fiacre was an Irish monk who travelled for Christ. In 630 he finally settled in France, and was, oddly, to give his name to the French hackney carriages which plied their trade from the Hôtel St Fiacre in Paris. His cult was at Meaux, in the neighbourhood of which he had made his hermitage. There in 670 he died and was buried.

In the seventeenth and eighteenth centuries Meaux became an important goal of pilgrimages. That was fitting, for a twelfth-century life of the saint claims that Fiacre built the first hostel for Irish pilgrims on the Continent, and that he planted a vegetable garden to sustain his guests.

AIDAN 31 August

In 635, at the request of Oswald (5 August), Aidan, an Irish monk, descended from the same line as Brigid (1 February) and originally attached to the community on Scattery Island, left Iona to preach the gospel to the Anglians of Northumberland. After the failure of Corman, his ascerbic predecessor as a missionary from Iona to Northumberland, Aidan was determined to use a gentle approach and one that was in any case more fitting to his kindly and humble nature.

When he arrived in Oswald's kingdom, with a group of companions from Iona, he set about establishing his monastery on a similar off-shore island, choosing the basaltic rocks of Lindisfarne, which are totally cut off from the mainland at high tide. Once he was established there, he was joined by more Celtic monks, but Anglo-Saxons also came to be trained in his monastery. One of his pupils was Chad (2 March), whom he later sent to finish his education in Ireland.

In the Celtic tradition, Aidan spent part of each year in solitude, choosing to retreat for the whole of Lent to the storm-tossed island of Inner Farne, now approachable by boat from Seahouses. It was while he was there one year, that he looked across to the mainland and saw flames pouring out of Oswald's castle at Bamburgh. Realizing that it was Penda's army that had set fire to the building he called down the wrath of God on the Mercians. Immediately the wind changed, sending the flames towards the attackers.

For Aidan, Lindisfarne was largely a centre from which he could set out on his missionary journeys, which consisted of walking round the countryside, talking to the people and doing all in his power to free the Celts still held as slaves by the conquering Angles. The King, who was much moved by this action of Aidan's, was himself of an extremely generous disposition. One Easter when King and Bishop were about to dine most sumptuously, they had not finished saying the grace to bless the food, when a servant whose duty it was to distribute alms to the poor came to announce that there was a great crowd of beggars outside the palace. Immediately Oswald sent all the food out to them; and Aidan delighting at that deed blessed the King, taking his right hand and declaring that it would never wither with age. His prophecy came true for, when Oswald was killed, his hand and arm were taken to Bamburgh and preserved in the reliquary there.

Aidan was at Lindisfarne for sixteen years. On the last day of August in 651, he was taken ill at Bamburgh and died in a makeshift shelter attached to the west side of the church. A pillar in the present church, which is dedicated to him, marks the place where he died. At the moment of his death, Cuthbert (20 March) looking after a flock of sheep on the Lammermuir Hills saw a vision of angels taking Aidan's soul to heaven.

AUGUST PILGRIMAGE

Cenydd's Cell, Burry Holms

The high tide island of Burry Holms is just off the north-western tip of Gower. If you go to the church at Llangennith, where Cenydd made his first settlement after leaving the monastic college at Llanilltud Fawr, you will find displayed the whole story of Cenydd's birth and miraculous survival. From here take the lane north-west to Broughton Burrows and start a lovely walk through flower-filled sand dunes to Burry Holms. *On no account try to cross to the island until the tide is well out* – there are treacherous quicksands here, and a murderous current round the rock. At low tide you can pick your way safely. You will find two ruins at

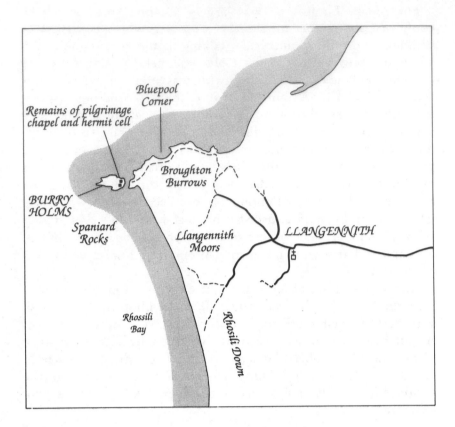

the eastern end of the island: one is Cenydd's hermit's cell, the other is the remains of a chapel or hostel for the pilgrims who came here in the Middle Ages.

 # September

Angels and Soul Friends

With the feast of Michael the Archangel falling on 29 September, and with Michaelmas daisies already in bloom, it is fitting that we should take the Celtic vision of angels and the corresponding notion of soul friends as our theme for this month. Angels are messengers from the other world, and in the Celtic tradition Michael had a particular importance for the dying. An eighth-century manuscript describes him as 'the leader of all souls to the throne of the Most High'; and a rosary of Michael for the dying collected by Diarmuid O'Laoghaire SJ makes this clear:

> Michael take him (her) in your hand
> And make his (her) peace with God's Son
> And if pursued by any enemy
> Do you place Christ between us and him.

In his contribution to James P. Mackey's *Introduction to Celtic Christianity*, O'Laoghaire points out that Father Allan MacDonald told Alexander Carmichael when the latter was collecting songs and prayers of the Highlands and Islands that 'The religious functions most commonly assigned by the people here [at Benbecula] to St Michael are his meeting of the souls of the elect at the moment of death, and his presiding at the balance where the soul's good and bad deeds are weighed'. This is reflected in this hymn for the dying, contained in Carmichael's *Carmina Gaedelica* (Oliver & Boyd, 1900), one of several in which Michael is invoked:

> And may Michael white kindly,
> High king of the holy angels,
> Take possession of the beloved soul,
> And shield it home to the Three of surpassing love,
>   Oh! to the Three of surpassing love.

Small wonder then that over and over again we find accounts

of angelic visions appearing to foretell the death of a particularly saintly person. Bede tells us how such a vision, accompanied with 'the sound of sweet and joyful singing coming down from heaven to earth' was experienced by the monk Owini of Lastingham just before the death of Chad. When he spoke of it to the bishop, Chad, who was aware of his coming death, explained to Owini that he had indeed encountered 'angelic spirits, who came to summon me to the heavenly reward that I have always hoped and longed for'.

Angels also have an important role as guides to the living, and the Celts held strongly to the belief that every soul from birth to death has its attendant guardian angel. A Breton prayer recorded as late as 1967 addresses such a guardian:

> My good angel, messenger of God,
> Protect my body and my soul;
> Protect me from the evil spirit
> And above all else from sin.

A section of St Patrick's breastplate, translated by N.D. O'Donoghue calls for:

> strong powers of the seraphim
> with angels obeying,
> and archangel attending,
> in the glorious company
> of the holy and risen ones.

I find a strong connection between the concept of the guardian angel and that of a living, human soul friend, the Celtic *Anamachara*, whose role might embrace that of confessor and spiritual director, but which was even more constant, intimate and confidential. The notion of the soul friend is one that came to the Celtic church through Egypt and North Africa, for the fourth-century John Cassian, whose writing were much referred to two hundred years later, spent time with the desert fathers and devoted one of his Conferences to friendship. And about the same time as Cassian was writing, St Augustine of Hippo suggested in one of his letters to a friend that the correspondence should be used 'as an invisible bridge to cross over and proceed in thought into my heart, and see what goes on there concerning you'.

Both angels and soul friends link the invisible to the visible world, and individual spirits with one another. This is independent of chronological time, for it is possible for a person to have a soul friend who is no longer inhabiting the material world. In the same way, angels, inhabiting the timeless other world, bridge spirit and matter. N.D. O'Donoghue makes their position in a Celtic church growing out of druidic beliefs quite sure, when he says 'The link here with pre-Christian animism and the fairy world of Celtic folk imagination is clear, and only those who wish to break all continuity between "paganism" and Christianity would wish to deny it'. We must always remember that the Celtic fairies, inhabitants of the grassy barrows of a vanished people, were as far removed from the tinsel of the Victorian imagination as their angels were from the decorative creatures portrayed in the stained glass of Burne-Jones. The angels the Celtic saints saw in their visions brought them a sense of awe and of the numinous, and their soul friendships grew out of courage and commitment.

SILYN   1 September

A sixth-century Irish monk who made his hermitage by the River Clyddach, which flows through Brechfa Forest in mid-Wales, Silyn is still remembered at the healing well near the village of Gwernogle (the place of the adders). There he is said to have saved a stag from the hunters, and to have given his name to a plant, Silyn's herb, a variety of plantain.

DRYCTHELM   1 September

At the monastery of old Melrose, in a bend of the River Tweed, at the end of the seventh century, a monk lived in virtual isolation, cut off from the rest of the community in order to devote himself more constantly to prayer. No matter how cold it was, he would spend a part of each day standing in the river reciting the psalms. His name was Drycthelm and, some years before, he had mysteriously returned to life after he had been pronounced dead.

Bede tells us that at the time of his first death, Drycthelm was a devout layman, the head of a Northumbrian household. When he miraculously returned to life, only his wife, who loved him dearly, remained beside him. The rest of the mourners fled in terror. As soon as he had recovered sufficiently, Drycthelm told her that he must now alter his way of life completely. So he divided his property three ways, giving one share to his beloved wife, another to his children and a third to the poor. He then retired to Melrose.

Later he was to speak of a vision he had experienced as he was led through scenes of judgement, hell and purgatory by his guide, 'a handsome man in a shining robe', who permitted him to have an intimation of heaven. Like others who report on a near–death experience, Drycthelm was reluctant to return to his body, claiming, as Bede reports, that he was 'entranced by the pleasantness and beauty' that he had glimpsed.

He never spoke of his vision to people who were simply curious or whom he feared might regard his experience in a superficial way as a subject of curiosity. To those who had thought deeply about the after-life, he would speak freely.

Father, bless to me my body,
Father, bless to me my soul,
Father, bless to me my life,
Father, bless to me my belief.

Collected by Alexander Carmichael

MACNISS 3 September

A hermit of Kells, Macniss lived in the latter part of the sixth century. Tradition claims that he was baptized by Patrick (17 March) and educated by Olcan (4 February). His miracles began even before he entered the church, for when his mother slapped him for going to sleep when he should have been watching her cattle, her whole arm went rigid.

As a priest, Macniss was to save the child of a patricide, doomed by rough Irish justice to lose his own son. The saint adopted the child and brought him up to be a leader of the church.

Macniss is said to have had such reverence for the gospel books, that he went down on all fours, carrying the manuscripts on his shoulders, rather than submit the heavy volumes to the indignity of being strapped on his back for carriage.

MONESSA 4 September

The beautiful daughter of an Irish prince, Monessa was so moved
when she heard Patrick preach that she sought immediate baptism.
Her joy was then so great that, overcome by it, she died.

Smooring*

> The sacred Three
> To save,
> To shield,
> To surround
> The hearth,
> The house,
> The household,
> This eve,
> This night,
> Oh! this eve,
> This night,
> And every night,
> Each single night.
>   Amen.

Collected by Alexander Carmichael

BEGA (BEE) 6 September

St Bee's on the Cumbrian coast is dedicated to Bega, friend and
disciple of Hilda (17 November), who was venerated for her
austerity, charity, and care for everyone with whom she came
into contact. It is said that when the monastery, of which she
was to become Abbess, was being built, she prepared and served
the builders' food herself. Some scholars identify her with Hein,
whom Aidan (31 August) placed at the head of the first nunnery
in the north of England.

Legend makes Bega out to be the daughter of an Irish king,
the most beautiful woman in the country, and courted by the

* To bank up a peat fire in such a way that it smoulders gently through
the night.

King of Norway. She, however, had already received a gift from the angels, a bracelet marked with the sign of the cross. This convinced her that she was called to serve God as a celibate; and so on the very day of her wedding, she withdrew from the crowds, sat alone on the grass and was miraculously transported to Northumbria. There she lived as a forest hermit, caring for the poor and the sick.

CAGNOLD   6 September

Born into a French noble family, Cagnold has his place in this calendar as the constant companion of Columbanus (21 November). He became the Irishman's pupil at Luxeuil and, having followed him into exile, was with him when he made his foundation at Bobbio. After Columbanus died in 615, Cagnold returned to Luxeuil and in 623 became Bishop of Laon.

DISIBOD   8 September

A seventh-century Irish bishop who travelled to the Continent, Disibod founded the monastery near Bingen which is associated with the twelfth-century mystic and polymath, Hildegarde. In 1170 she wrote a life of the founder of her community based on a vision which she had of him.

CIERAN   9 September

The son of a travelling carpenter, and descended through his mother from a national bard, Cieran was born at Connaught. As a lad he was taught by Finnian of Clonard (12 December) and later he went to join Enda (21 March) on the Aran Islands, where he was ordained priest. He spent seven years there, seeing to the threshing of the corn grown by the community, before leaving to start his own foundations. The first of these, of which he became abbot, was on an island on Lough Ree. There he stayed for a further seven years.

In 548 he moved to the west bank of the Shannon, where he founded the monastery of Clonmacnoise, whose ruins still stand among several medieval churches. He was only to be there for

Clonmacnoise

seven months, for at the early age of thirty-three he contracted plague and died.

It is recorded in the *Book of Lismore* that his brilliance had caused such jealousy among his colleagues that 'all the other saints of Ireland fasted against him, praying that he would die young'. Even Kevin (3 June) who attended him on his death-bed, and Columcille (9 June) seem to have been glad of his death, for the latter is quoted as exclaiming 'Blessing on God who took this holy Cieran! For if he had remained until he was an ancient man, he would not have found the place of two chariot horses in Ireland that would not have been his.'

Despite that remark, Columcille wrote one of his hymns in praise of Cieran, and is said to have taken a sod of earth from his grave back to Iona, and always travelled with it. Once when he was caught in the fearsome whirlpool of Corryvrechan, he cast it into the sea, and at once the waters calmed.

FINNIAN OF MOVILLE   10 September

Educated at the monastic college of Whithorn in Galloway (*see* Ninian, 26 August), Finnian, an Irishman of royal birth, went back to his native land to found the monastery at Moville, County Down, in the middle of the sixth century. There Columcille (9 June) became one of his many disciples.

DEINIOL   11 September

Descended from a Celtic chieftain in north Britain, Deiniol, born in the first part of the sixth century, founded the North Wales coastal monastery of Bangor. The foundation was to become so important that Bede was able to claim that by 603 it had over two thousand monks, twelve hundred of whom were to lose their lives at the Battle of Chester, fighting against the pagan Aethelfrith of Northumbria.

In Rygyvarch's life of David, Deiniol and Dyfrig (14 November) were named as the two bishops who were the prime organizers of the Synod of Llanddewi Brefi (*see* David, 1 March).

Apologia pro Vita Sua

I read or write, I teach or wonder what is truth,
    I call upon my God by night and day.
I eat and freely drink, I make my rhymes,
    And snoring sleep, or vigil keep and pray.
And very 'ware of all my shames I am;
    O Mary, Christ, have mercy on your man.

Translated by Helen Waddell

AILBE   12 September

The story goes that Ailbe, the son of a slave girl, was left on a hillside to die as soon as he was born. There a she-wolf found him and carried him gently to her lair to bring him up with her cubs. Before many days had gone by he was found and adopted by a hunter, but he never forgot the wolf who had saved his life. Years later, having been baptized and ordained bishop, he was able to save the life of his wolf foster-mother when she was being hunted. Thereafter she came every day to the hall where he was dining, and in his turn he fed her.

Ailbe, as bishop, obtained the gift of an Aran island for Enda (21 March) from King Angus of Munster. His own foundation was at Munster, 10 miles (16 km) to the west of Tipperary. According to the Ulster annals, Ailbe died in 527, having been privileged while still alive to have a glimpse of the Islands of the Blessed.

Ailbe

I Weave Till Dawn

Warp on the woof
I weave till dawn,
    Love,
By the sheiling.
Warp on the woof,
    Love,
I weave till dawn.

Blue on the green,
Like the dew on the grass,
    Love,
By the sheiling.
Blue on the green,
    Love,
I weave till dawn.

Kenneth Macleod

MIRIN 15 September

The ruins of a chapel dedicated to the Irish Mirin can be found on the largest island in Loch Lomond, which bears the saint's name. He is reputed to have been a disciple of Comgall (11 May) and to have become a monk at Bangor (County Down) before crossing to Scotland where he founded the monastery at Paisley, where he died and was buried. His shrine was for a long time a focus of pilgrimages.

Protection

May God shield me,
May God fill me,
May God keep me,
May God watch me.

May God bring me
    To the land of peace,
    To the country of the King,
        To the peace of eternity.

Collected by Alexander Carmichael

Sleep

I lie down to-night
With fair Mary and with her Son,
With pure-white Michael,
And with Bride beneath her mantle.

Collected by Alexander Carmichael

LOLAN   22 September

A nephew of Serf (1 July), Lolan is said to have been born at Cana in Galilee, and to have worked and studied in Rome for seven years. At the end of that time, longing to see his uncle, he set out to walk to Scotland, having left the key to the sacristy of St Peter's Basilica where his successor might find it.

A story in the Aberdeen Breviary recounts that Lolan had not gone very far on his journey when the Deacon and Sub-deacon of St Peter's came after him complaining that no hand but his could turn the key in the lock. Thereupon Lolan cut off his right hand and gave it to the prelates, asking only in return that he be sent four loads of earth from the cemetery in Rome in which to be buried.

ADOMNAN   23 September

Soul friend to Finnacha, King of Ireland, Adomnan was born in 624 and became Abbot of Iona at the age of fifty-five. In 688 he was sent to Northumbria to negotiate the exchange of some Irish captives, and while he was there lodged with Coelfrid, Abbot of Wearmouth, who converted him to the Roman rule. Unable to persuade the monks of Iona to his way of thinking, Adomnan left the Abbey and went back to Ireland, but returned to die amongst his still obdurate monks in 705.

Adomnan is chiefly remembered for his two books: a travelogue and a biography. The former is an account of a visit to Jerusalem, Alexandria and Constantinople undertaken by Arculf, a Frankish bishop, who was shipwrecked on the way home, blown off course and who landed on Iona. There he dictated his adventures to the abbot. The biography is the much-prized life of Columcille (9 June) and was written at the request of the monks of Iona, sometime before Adomnan went to Wearmouth.

A lover of peace, Adomnan set himself against the Celtic tribal custom of sending women and children into battle; and he also claimed that clerics should be exempt from serving as soldiers.

MAWGAN   24 September

A Welsh monk, possibly abbot of a settlement in Pembrokeshire, Mawgan crossed the Channel with Brioc (1 May). In Cornwall he is associated with Mawgan-in-Meneage, 4 miles (6 km) south-east of Helston; and in the north of the county, near Newquay, the Vale of Mawgan bears his name. In that latter place is the church of Mawgan-in-Pydar. The oldest part of the present building is its thirteenth-century tower, but the church is said to stand on the site of a Celtic monastery.

FINBAR   25 September

A native of Connaught, the blind Finbar (whose real name was Lochan) was to be known by his nickname, which means the white-haired. His father was a metal-worker, and like all smiths held in almost superstitious awe. His mother was a slave girl. He grew up to become a friend of David (1 March) and to become the founder and first bishop of the see of Cork in 600. He was also the patron of Barra in the Outer Hebrides, where he spent some time as a hermit.

CADOC   25 September

Son of Gwladys, the eldest daughter of Brychan (6 April), and Gwynllyw (29 March), a chieftain of Glamorgan, the sixth-century Cadoc spent some years studying in Ireland as a young man. On his return he converted his parents to an austere Christian life, and established his own monastery at Llancarfan, some 10 miles (16 km) south-west of Cardiff.

Finnian of Clonard (12 December) became his pupil, joining him on the Bristol Channel island of Flat Holm, where he was wont to have a hermitage. Lifris, one of Cadoc's biographers, tells us that the rocks around that island, known as the wolves, were wolves in fact, turned to stone when they tried to swim across the water after Cadoc's sheep.

Sometime in the 560s, Cadoc travelled to Scotland, and it is said that he founded a monastery to the west of Stirling, where Machan (28 September) became one of his disciples. There is a church dedicated to him at Cambuslang in the Clyde Valley.

In old age Cadoc travelled north from Glamorgan to the banks of the River Usk as it flows to the south of the Black Mountains; there he is remembered in the church of Llangattock (the *llan* of Cadoc) near Crickhowell. Our knowledge of his life comes from two twelfth-century hagiographers: Caradoc, a Brecon-born hermit of Gower; and Lifris, a monk of Llancarfan, who seems to have confused the Welsh founder of his monastery with a Breton saint of the same name.

BARUC 27 September

A disciple of Cadoc (25 September) and variously known as Barrok or Barry, Baruc became a hermit on the island off the coast from Cardiff, which now bears a version of his name. He is reported to have died there and many pilgrimages were made to his chapel which in the sixteenth century was the only building on the island. Another tradition, recorded by William Worcester, claims that he is buried at Fowey in Cornwall.

MACHAN 28 September

In Glasgow Cathedral there is an altar in honour of this sixth-century saint, an Irishman, consecrated bishop in Rome, who worked mainly in Campsie where he is buried.

MICHAEL 29 September

Michael the Victorious

Thou Michael the Victorious
I make my circuit under thy shield,
Thou Michael of the white steed,
And of the bright brilliant blades,
Conqueror of the dragon,
Be thou at my back,
Thou ranger of the heavens,
Thou warrior of the King of all,
    O Michael the victorious
    My pride and my guide,
    O Michael the victorious
    The glory of mine eye.

I make my circuit
In the fellowship of the saint,
On the machair,* on the meadow,
On the cold heathery hill;
Though I should travel ocean
And the hard globe of the world
No harm can ever befall me
'Neath the shelter of thy shield;
    O Michael the victorious,
    Jewel of my heart,
    O Michael the victorious,
    God's shepherd thou art.

Be the sacred Three of Glory
Aye at peace with me,
With my horses, with my cattle,
With my woolly sheep in flocks.
With the crops growing in the field
Or ripening in the sheaf,
On the machair, on the moor,
In cole, in heap, or stack.
    Every thing on high or low,
    Every furnishing and flock,
    Belong to the holy Triune of glory,
    And to Michael the Victorious.

Collected by Alexander Carmichael

* Machair: grass sward by the ocean

SEPTEMBER PILGRIMAGE

Cieran's monastery, Clonmacnoise

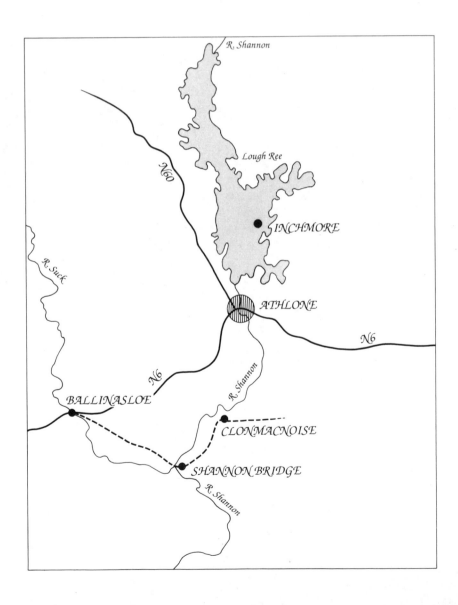

Cieran's monastery of Clonmacnoise on the banks of the Shannon, to the south of Athlone, is an uninhabited city of holy ruins and carved stones. Once one of the chief monasteries and colleges of Ireland, the ancient walls of Clonmacnoise, its high crosses and plundered shrines still attract thousands of pilgrims each year. Services are frequently held here.

 # October

The Celtic Vision

Time and again we read in the lives of the Celtic saints how the timeless world impinges on this one in the form of angelic visions, such as we thought about in September. Now, as the Celtic year comes to its close, I want to look at vision in a slightly different context and consider the Celtic view of this world and the next.

In the sixty-eighth chapter of his complaint about the state of the nation, Gildas lamented that, although Britain had priests, they were 'insipientes', a word which has been translated as foolish, but which is far nearer to the Latin sense of being lukewarm, indifferent and above all unaware. For the Celts, as for the Buddhists, sin consists largely in being uncaring and heedless. To live truly is to live with mindfulness, to keep your eyes open.

To begin with, we need to be aware of the place that we inhabit, the stretch of land we walk over, and from that look to the whole of natural creation. I am grateful to William Parker Marsh and Christopher Bamford (*Celtic Christianity: Ecology and Holiness*), for reminding me that early in the twentieth century H.J. Massingham, a great writer on farming and rural life, declared that 'If the British Church had survived, it is possible that the fissure between Christianity and nature, widening through the centuries, would not have cracked the unity of western man's attitude to the universe'. Massingham must have been aware that the Celtic church was rooted in rural communities, whereas the Roman rule that superceded it belonged more to the hierarchies of the cities. The structure of the communities which formed the Celtic Christian tribes and monasteries was, in the terms used by Matthew Fox and outlined in his *Creation Spirituality* (Harper Collins, 1991), more aligned to the mode of a circle dance than to that of climbing a ladder. The latter model is based on competition and hierarchies, while to dance in a circle is to acknowledge the feminine and to be 'close to the earth, egalitarian, self-healing, self-motivating and self-organising like the universe itself'.

In the Celtic vision an awareness of this world is always combined with intimations of eternity, which was often envisaged as an island of the blessed, lying far out across the western sea. Sometimes in the druidic imagination, souls were carried there in a ship of white crystal. More dreadfully, the damned would have to make the journey in the fearful longtheine, the fire ship. Kenneth Macleod in *The Road to the Isles* told how the people of his native island of Eigg claimed to have seen such a vessel, and declared that 'on the deck was a long, lean, black creature, with a fiddle in his hand, and he ever playing and dancing and laughing – and O St Mary and my love, awful was the howling that was below'. This spectre, seen by those cursed with the second sight (the vision of the other world imposed on this one, and of the past or future imposed on the present), is a reminder to us that demons were as real to the Celtic imagination as angels. Only an insipid fool would turn a blind eye to evil and neglect to take the necessary steps to protect himself from it.

We find such calls for protection in St Patrick's breastplate, and in the *Caim* or encircling prayers intended to draw a line of power and strength around a person, which no evil force could penetrate. Esther de Waal in *The Celtic Vision* tells us that such an imaginary circle was drawn 'by stretching out the right hand with the forefinger extended and turning sunwise, as though on a pivot, so that the circle enclosed and accompanied the man or woman as they walked, and safeguarded them from all evil, within and without'. She drew that description from the writings of Alexander Carmichael, and she goes on to give several examples of the encompassing prayers that he collected, and which would have been intoned as the circle was drawn. Here is one of them:

> The compassing of God and His right hand
> Be upon my form and upon my frame;
> The compassing of the High King and the grace of the Trinity
> Be upon me abiding ever eternally,
>   Be upon me abiding ever eternally.

The *Caim* reminds us how the Celts, in all sorts of ways, used ritual to enhance their awareness of both the natural and the supernatural world. It is a trait that comes partly from the druidic tradition, which relied entirely on the spoken rather than the written word to pass on its teachings; and partly from the seasonal rites of the natural year and the course of human life. These rituals are embodied in the songs and poems that Alexander Carmichael collected in the Scottish Highlands. From them we learn how a love of ritual and liturgical repetitive words links the druidic tradition to the Celtic church. Indeed, the sixth-century Welsh bard, Taliesin, (*see* Introduction, p. 7) declared that there never was a time when the Druids of Britain did not hold to the doctrines of Christianity.

The constant awareness of nature, of the interaction between men and women and the spiritual world, and of the eternal presence of God the creator, is also always apparent in Celtic art. Small animals find a place among heraldic beasts in the decorations that surround the text; and the involved, convoluted knotwork painted on manuscript pages and carved on stone crosses is always a configuration of the eternal. The spiritual is unending, and interwoven with every aspect of daily life. As Esther de Waal has put it, the Celts 'made no distinction between the secular and the sacred. They were unable to discern boundaries of where religion began and ended and thus found it natural to assume that God was lovingly concerned in everything they did. They felt totally at home with God.'

MYLOR　1 October

An obscure saint of uncertain date and probably of Breton origin, Mylor is chiefly associated with Amesbury, which acquired his relics; but he is also remembered in three Cornish churches: Mylor, Merther Myle and Linkinhorn.

The medieval legends tell us that as a child of seven he was almost murdered by an uncle, who had just killed his father. Dissuaded by a council of bishops from slaughtering his nephew, the uncle contented himself with cutting off the child's right hand and left foot. These were replaced by metal appendages, which as the lad grew eventually became flesh and blood. This so infuriated the uncle that he persuaded the boy's guardian to commit murder. This he did by striking off Mylor's head. In his delight the uncle picked up the severed head and died three days later. Mylor's body was taken to Amesbury, from whence it could never be removed.

MURDACH   5 October

The last of the bards, Murdach lived as a hermit near a lake in Argyleshire. Dempster, who compiled the Scottish *Menology* (Calendar of Saints), and from whom we have our sole knowledge of this undated saint, refers to him as a Culdee, which would probably take him into the eighth century or later.

CUMINE   6 October

Distantly related through his paternal grandfather to Columcille (9 June), Cumine was elected Abbot of Iona in 657 and ruled for twelve years. A life of Columcille in 134 chapters has been attributed to him.

YWI   8 October

Son of Bran, a Celtic chief, Ywi was born near Lindisfarne and became a disciple of Cuthbert (20 March). Wishing to follow the Irish example of travelling for Christ without any fixed destination, he boarded a ship setting sail from the coast of Northumbria. Some accounts have it that he died during a storm at sea off the Breton coast; others affirm that he reached Brittany safely and lived the austere life of a hermit there. Whatever the case, his relics were brought to Wilton near Salisbury by some travelling Breton monks in the ninth century. They did not intend to leave them there, but found, that by some miraculous intervention, it was impossible to carry the bones away.

KEYNE   8 October

A daughter or grand-daughter of Brychan (6 April), Keyne's birth was heralded by a vision in which her mother saw rays of light shooting from her breast as she nursed a dove in her lap. As a little girl, the lovely Keyne was sometimes as radiant as the sun, sometimes as pure white as snow. She grew up to be very beautiful.

When she decided to dedicate her life to God, rather than choose marriage, she left her home in Wales, crossing the Severn Estuary

St Keyne's Well

and settling in the area between Bath and Bristol, now known as Keynsham. The many large ammonite fossils discovered in the limestone there gave rise to the belief that the place was once infected with snakes, all of which Keyne turned to stone.

While she was there, Cadoc (25 September), reputed to be her nephew, visited her on his way to Cornwall; although another account tells us that she met him at Mount St Michael, near Penzance. Whatever actually happened, it seems certain that Cadoc persuaded his aunt to return to her own country and to settle near Abergavenny, where there is still a spring dedicated to her. On the day of her death a column of fire was seen over her cell, where she lay on a bed of bracken. Her biographies tell us that two angels then came to her and, taking off her sackcloth habit, clothed her in crimson and gold for her entry to heaven.

The suggestion that at sometime in her life she visited Cornwall is substantiated by the well near Liskeard that bears her name. The property of its waters is is to give dominance in marriage to whichever spouse manages to get a drink of it first. Hence Robert Southey's verse;

> I hasten'd as soon as the wedding was o'er
> And left my good wife in the porch,
> But i' faith she had been wiser than I
> For she took a bottle to church.

TRIDUNA   8 October

There are many versions of Triduna's name, so I have kept to the Latin of the Aberdeen Breviary; however it is as well to be aware that she is also known as Trallew, Trallen, and in the *Orkneyinga Saga* as Trollhaena. It was she, accompanied by Regulus or Rule (17 October), who came from Constantinople in 397, bearing the relics of St Andrew the apostle to Scotland. There she settled as a hermit, first at Rescoby in Forfarshire, then in Dunfallandy in Atholl, and finally at Restalrig in Lothian.

During the course of these wanderings, she is said to have plucked out her eyes, presenting them on a thorn to an unwanted suitor, who had claimed that he was bound to die for love of her beautiful eyes. After her death, at Restalrig, where an image of the saint is shown with a thorn transfixing her eye sockets, people sought her intercession for poor sight. So many pilgrims visited her shrine that at the Reformation it was declared that 'the kirk at Restalrig, a monument of idolatory, be raysit and utterlie cast down and destroyed'.

The site of her well at Restalrig has since been excavated, and it was discovered that the spring was once covered by a two-storey building containing a chapel and a piscina. Triduna also has a shrine on Papa Westwray in the Orkneys, on a rock beside the loch that bears her name.

PAULINUS OF YORK   10 October

A Roman monk who came to Kent with St Augustine, Paulinus takes his place in a Celtic calendar because of the influence he had on Hilda (17 November), who was baptized by him at the royal palace of Yeavering in Northumbria, where he conducted mass conversions.

KENNETH (CANICE)   11 October

An Irish Pict, born around 516 in Keenaght, County Derry, Kenneth was the son of a bard, who sent him to Clonard to be educated by Finnian (12 December). Later he was to go for a short while to Wales, to study under Cadoc (25 September) at Llancarfan.

A friend of Columcille (9 June), and like him included as one of the Twelve Apostles of Ireland, Kenneth sailed for Scotland in 562 and, being a Pict, had an especially important role to play in Columcille's missionary journey to King Brude of Inverness.

Adomnan (23 September), who wrote a life of Columcille, tells of several incidents proving the clear telepathic communion between the two men. One concerns Kenneth's crozier (a staff made of a long-shafted cross) left behind on Iona. Columcille went to the oratory to pray about this, a good example of the way that in the Celtic tradition every detail of daily life was referred to God, and being assured that his friend would call at Islay, left it there on the turf above the beach where Kenneth would be sure to find it.

Two other incidents were occasioned by storms at sea. In the first, on a day of 'crashing tempest and terrible rising of the waves', Columcille told his incredulous monks that they would shortly receive a guest from Ireland and must make haste to prepare for him. As soon as the storm died down, Kenneth landed on Iona.

The second incident took place when Kenneth was in Ireland at the monastery which he had established at Aghaboe, sometime before 577. On that occasion Columcille was actually at sea when the storm blew up. Immediately he told his companions that Kenneth would pray for them. Sure enough, at that very moment, in the refectory with his monks, Kenneth heard the voice of Columcille and left the table, pausing only to latch one sandal. With his monks he hurried into the oratory to pray for the Abbot of Iona. As he was doing so, Columcille told his terrified shipmates that they had no cause for fear for 'God has looked on the zeal of Kenny, running to church with only one shoe on his foot, to pray for us'.

In Scotland, Kenneth had his own settlement on the island that bears his name, to the north of Iona. Now there are only sheep on Inch Kenneth, but in the Middle Ages, a chapel, now in ruins, was built on the site of Kenneth's oratory and drew many pilgrims across the water from Mull. In 1773, Dr Johnson, sixty-four years old and seriously failing in health, came here with Boswell, daring

Kenneth (Canice)

the rough seas in a frail craft. He found Inch Kenneth to be 'a proper prelude to Iona' and by the roofless chapel he wrote some Latin verses in honour of the saint.

From his island settlement, Kenneth made many missionary journeys on his own account. He is remembered in the Outer Hebrides at Colonsay, Tiree and Lochboisdale; while on the mainland to the east he is associated with the hillside above Kinloch Laggan, beneath the southern slopes of the forbidding, grey Monadhliath Mountains. There he established a settlement which for a short while rivalled Iona in the numbers of people who were drawn to it.

In Ireland, Kenneth is remembered for the work he undertook as a scribe. At his monastery at Aghaboe (now known as Kilkenny), which was to become the residence of the Bishops of Ossory, he made copies of the four gospels, to which he added his own commentaries. The work was known as the *Chain of Canice*.

He was also renowned for his affinity with animals, which apparently gave force to the discipline with which he controlled them, expelling mice from his cell because they nibbled his shoes, and demanding that the birds stop singing on Sundays.

FIECH   12 October

A disciple of the druidic bard Dubtach, the father of Brigid (1 February), Fiech was a harper and singer, who according to tradition was baptized and eventually became a bishop.

COMGAN   13 October

Son of Kelly, Prince of Leinster, Comgan was driven out of his territory by hostile neighbouring tribes, and forced to seek asylum in Scotland. There he lived for a while with his sister and her children, one of whom was Fillan (9 January). Eventually he founded a small monastery at Lochalsh, across the water from Skye. When he died there, Fillan took his body to Iona for burial and built a church in his honour.

LEVAN   14 October

A patron of St Levan in Cornwall, this sixth-century monk was probably a Welshman on his way to Brittany, and has been identified with a saint of the same name, who is honoured in southern Brittany. He is supposed to have spent some time as a hermit on the cliff by St Levan, at a place where a chapel was later to be built.

His chief characteristic seems to have been his delight in fishing. The carved bench-ends in St Levan church record the best-known angler's tale connected with this saint. Here you will find a carving of two fish on one hook. It commemorates the time when, so it is said, he landed two bream with one cast. He threw both fish back into the sea, but when he cast again the same thing happened. When this incident had been repeated three times, he decided to take the fish home. There he found that he had unexpected guests, for his sister Breage and her two children had come to visit him. The apparently God-given food should have been a great blessing, but the story goes that the hungry children ate too quickly and choked on the fish bones. This gave rise to another version of the tale, which explains that Levan's catch was not bream, but chad, a coarse fish thought to be fit only for children, but being full of bones, it was called 'chuck-cheeld' or 'choke child' by the St Levan fishermen.

In 1740, the Reverend Dr William Borlaise, a Cornish antiquarian and parson, was told about several pieces of folklore centring on the saint by the landlady of an inn near St Levan. One story concerned the way the saint had cursed the name Johanna, because a woman of that name rebuked him for going fishing on a Sunday, while she was herself profaning the Sabbath by gathering pot herbs for her dinner. Levan decreed that any child to be christened with that name in water from his well would grow up to be a great fool. Thus all the records of Johanna baptisms are in the neighbouring parish of Sennen.

Dr Borlaise also learnt of the local belief that any consistent stretch of very green grass indicated that the saint had taken that path on his way to go fishing. Finally Borlaise's landlady repeated the doggerel verse, which the saint is supposed to have uttered as a prophecy after he had cracked the boulder of granite on the south side of the church to the east of the porch. The lines run:

When the panniers astride
A pack-horse, can ride
Through St Levan's stone,
The world will be done.

GALL   16 October

A Leinster man, like Columbanus (21 November), Gall travelled with that great missionary across the Continent, by way of Annegray and Luxeuil to Tuggen (Lake Zurich). When they came to Arbon Forest, a wilderness south of Lake Constance, Gall fell sick and could or would not continue travelling, so Columbanus went on into Italy without him. This caused a bitter dispute between the two men, for Columbanus chose to believe that Gall's sickness was feigned and forbade his companion to celebrate Mass again so long as he (Columbanus) lived.

In fact Gall outlived his friend by some fifteen years, dying around 630. Having previously refused to become Abbot of Luxeuil, he lived the rest of his life as a hermit and itinerant preacher, taking the Arbon Forest as his base. About a hundred years after his death, a great abbey grew up on the site of his hermitage. It flourished until 1805 when it was dissolved by Napoleon.

In 1529, the shrine of St Gall in the monastery was broken into. The skeleton of a tall man was revealed, and beside the bones a Celtic belt and crozier. The latter is thought to have belonged to Columbanus who, as he lay dying in Bobbio, sent it to his old friend and companion as a token of his forgiveness.

REGULUS (RULE)   17 October

The Aberdeen Breviary tells us that Regulus was entrusted by an angel with the guardianship of the relics of St Andrew, and told that for their safety he should take these bones away from Patras in Archaia, the site of the Apostle's martyrdom, to some unrevealed destination. Regulus did as the angel bid, wandering across Europe with the precious relics until he came to north Britain. There in the Scottish town that now bears the Apostle's name, the angel appeared once more to Regulus and told him that this was the resting place for the holy relics. So Regulus settled there and became a missionary to the Picts.

WENNA   18 October

Founder of the church of St Wenn in north Cornwall, and sometimes referred to as Gwen of Cornwall, Wenna is believed to be another of the daughters of Brychan (6 April). She was married to Selyf, a king of Cornwall, and was mother of Cybi (8 November) and sister of Non (3 March). In south Cornwall the church at Morval near East Looe is dedicated to her.

ETHBIN   19 October

Born in Britain in the sixth century and educated by Samson (28 July), Ethbin became a monk in Brittany, where he was a disciple of Winwaloe (3 March). The last twenty years of his life were spent as a forest hermit in Ireland, but the location has not been identified.

The Care of Nature

It were as easy for Jesu
To renew the withered tree
As to wither the new
Were it His will to do so.
 Jesu! Jesu! Jesu!
 Jesu! meet it were to praise Him.

There is no plant in the ground
But it is full of His virtue,
There is no form in the strand
But it is full of His blessing.
 Jesu! Jesu! Jesu!
 Jesu! meet it were to praise Him.

There is no life in the sea,
There is no creature in the river,
There is naught in the firmament
But proclaims His goodness.
 Jesu! Jesu! Jesu!
 Jesu! meet it were to praise Him.

There is no bird on the wing,
There is no star in the sky,
There is nothing beneath the sun
But proclaims His goodness.
 Jesu! Jesu! Jesu!
 Jesu! meet it were to praise Him.

Collected by Alexander Carmichael

FINTAN MUNNU   21 October

A descendant of Niall of the Nine Hostages (*see* page 38),
Fintan was educated at Bangor under Comgall (11 May), before
becoming a disciple of Columcille (9 June), then still in Ireland.
Later, Fintan set out himself for Iona; but as he prepared to do
so he heard that Columcille had died. Nevertheless he resolved
to continue with his plans, only to find that the new Abbot of
Iona, Barthen, refused to admit him, claiming that before he died
Columcille had decreed that should Fintan come to Iona he was to
be told to go back to Ireland and establish a monastery in Leinster.
This must have occurred about 597. Fintan's main foundation was
to be at Taghmon in Wexford.

There is a tradition that Fintan contracted leprosy, and that for
twenty three years he used such self-control that he never scratched
his itching sores, or attended to them in any way, save that he
took a bath each Maundy Thursday. This penance he undertook
in order to merit the heavenly reward granted to his friend and
mentor Molua (4 August). The medieval life of Fintan declared
that on his death on this day in 635, as the angels carried his soul
away they met a gang of demons bent on destruction. When the
evil spirits saw Fintan's face, they were so awestruck that for seven
days they could do no harm.

TUDA   21 October

Immediately after the fateful Synod of Whitby (*see* page 38) which
was held at Easter in 664, the disappointed Colman (18 February)
left Northumbria for Iona, and Tuda became Bishop of Lindisfarne
in his place. At the beginning of May, Tuda succumbed to a fatal

attack of plague which, Bede tells us, followed an eclipse of the sun that occurred at ten o'clock in the morning on 3 May, 664.

DONATUS   22 October

An Irish monk who undertook a pilgrimage to Rome in the ninth century, Donatus became Bishop of Fiesole in 829. There he founded a hostel for Irish pilgrims, which he dedicated to Brigid (1 February), whose biography he had written. His other writings include a poem in praise of Ireland and his own epitaph.

A Poem by Columcille

That I might bless the Lord
Who conserves all,
Heaven with its countless bright orders,
Land, strand and flood.

MAGLORIUS   24 October

Of Irish origin, Maglorius was educated at Llantwit Major under Illtyd (6 November). He became a missionary with Samson (28 July) and journeyed with him to Brittany. Later he retired to Sark, where he founded a monastery at which he spent the rest of his life.

EATA   26 October

One of the twelve youths of Northumbria, chosen to be the first disciples of Aidan (31 August), Eata, according to Bede, was 'a meek and simple man'. He was to become the first Abbot of Melrose where he taught Cuthbert (20 March). After the Synod of Whitby in 678 he became Bishop of Hexham, a see to which he returned in 685, having spent the three years from 681 as Bishop of Lindisfarne.

ODHRAN 27 October

When Columcille (9 June) arrived on Iona, he found a Christian monastery there, directed by Odhran. This first settler appears to have joined the community founded by Columcille, who told his companions that whoever among them would be the first to die would confirm the Irish right to the island and be assured of an easy passage to heaven. Odhran, weary of the world, apparently consented to be the victim, and Columcille promised that in future years all intercessions must be made through him. The fact that Odhran was buried at the place where Columcille built his abbey is in keeping with that aspect of folklore which demands that a corpse (be it only that of a mummified cat) must be buried in the walls of any new building to ensure good fortune.

COLMAN MACDUACH 29 October

There are at least ninety-six Colmans recorded in Ireland; this one is best known for the story which opens the account of his life. It records that Colman MacDuach had three pets: a cock, a mouse and a fly. The crowing of the cock woke him in time for him to say his office; should he not then get up the mouse would nibble his fingers; and the fly served as a bookmark, settling at the end of the paragraph which the saint had finished reading. Distraught at the eventual death of his three friends, Colman wrote to Columcille on Iona, only to be rebuked for letting such trifles unsettle him. It seems an unduly harsh response, since Colman, who chose to live as a hermit under a cliff in the uncompromisingly harsh limestone landscape of the Burren in County Clare, was a man given to great austerity, existing on a diet of vegetables and water.

He died about 632, and in 780 Oengus the Culdee (11 March) instituted a pilgrimage to the rock-circled Valley of Oughtmama in the Burren, the place with which Colman was associated, and where a Cistercian monastery was established in 1195. Colman's crozier is in the National Museum in Dublin.

TALARICAN   30 October

A rare instance of a sixth-century Pictish saint, Talarican worked in the north of Scotland and is honoured in various churches in Aberdeen, Moray and Ross.

FOILLAN   30 October

A brother of Fursey (16 January), Foillan took over the care of the monastery at Burgh Castle in Suffolk after Fursey had gone to France. On Fursey's death in 650, Foillan and another of his brothers, Uttan, were invited to go to the Continent and establish a monastery at Fosses near Nivelles, Belgium, for the benefit of Irish immigrants.

It was in that region that Foillan was murdered, being set on by a band of brigands who threw his body into the thick undergrowth of the Forest of Soignies. In 1952 excavations at Fosses uncovered a Roman villa beneath the church attached to the Irish monastery, and also discovered that a small wooden oratory had once been attached to the church.

ERC   31 October

Patron of St Erth in Cornwall and referred to as the brother of Ia (3 February) and Euny, Erc was one of a group of Irish missionaries to land in the Hayle Estuary in north Cornwall. He is said to have been converted by Patrick (17 March).

At the Ending of the Day

I am lying down tonight as beseems
In the fellowship of Christ, son of the Virgin of ringlets,
In the fellowship of the gracious Father of glory,
In the fellowship of the Spirit of powerful aid.

I am lying down tonight with God,
And God tonight will lie down with me,
I will not lie down tonight with sin, nor shall
Sin or sin's shadow lie down with me.

I am lying down tonight with the Holy Spirit,
And the Holy Spirit this night will lie down with me,
I will lie down this night with the Three of my love,
And the Three of my love will lie down with me.

Collected by Alexander Carmichael

OCTOBER PILGRIMAGE

Foillan's Monastery, Burgh Castle, Suffolk

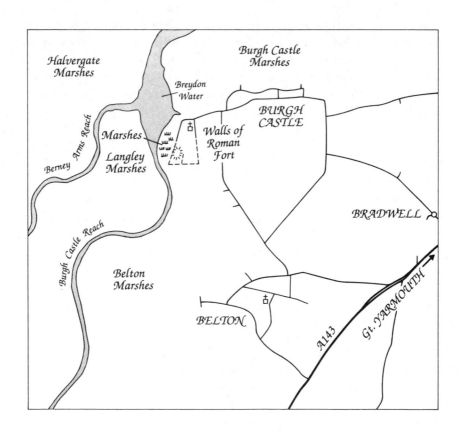

Ending the year's pilgrimages in the Saxon stronghold of East Anglia reminds us that early in the seventh century many descendants of Boudicca's tribe of the Iceni still lived in these parts. It also makes clear how widespread was the power of the Irish church. It is interesting that Foillan's brother Fursey (16 January) deliberately chose to make his settlement at the site of a Roman stronghold – for that is what you will find, its massive walls still standing, if you take the walk across the marshes from the church, which stands to the west of the village of Burgh Castle.

 # Bibliography

Baring-Gould, Sabine *The Lives of the British Saints*, in four volumes published between 1907–1913.

Bamford, Christopher and Marsh, William Parker *Celtic Christianity: Ecology and Holiness*, Floris Books, Edinburgh, 1986.

Bede *Ecclesiastical History of the English People*, translated by Leo Sherley-Price and revised by R.E. Latham, Penguin, 1990.

Bowen, E.G. *Saints, Seaways and Settlements in the Celtic Lands*, University of Wales Press, 1987.

Braz, Anatole le *The Land of Pardons*, Methuen, 1906.

Brown, Peter *The Book of Kells*, Thames and Hudson, 1989.

Campbell, Marion *Mid Argyll: A Handbook of History*, Natural History and Antiquarian Society of Mid Argyll, 1970.

Carmichael, Alexander *The Sun Dances: Prayers and Blessings from the Gaelic*, selected by Adam Bittleston, Floris Books, Edinburgh, 1960.

de Waal, Esther *A World Made Whole*, Fount, 1991.

—*The Celtic Vision: Selections from the Carmina Gadelica*, Darton, Longman & Todd, 1988.

—*God under my Roof*, SLG Press, Oxford, 1987.

Doble, G.H. *Lives of the Welsh Saints*, University of Wales Press, 1971.

—*The Saints of Cornwall*, Holywell Press, Oxford, 1970.

Ellis, Peter Beresford *The Cornish Saints*, Tor Mark Press, Penryn, 1992.

Farmer, David Hugh *The Oxford Dictionary of Saints*, Clarendon Press, 1978.

Gildas *The Ruin of Britain and Other Works*, edited and translated by Michael Winterton, Phillimore, 1978.

Giot, P.R., Fleuriot, L. and Bernier G. *Les Premiers Bretons*, Editions Jos le Doaré, 29150 Chateaulin, 1985.

Hanson, R.P.C. *Saint Patrick: His Origins and Career*, Clarendon Press, 1968.

Jackson, Kenneth Hurlestone *A Celtic Miscellany*, Penguin, 1971.

MacGowan, Kenneth *Glendaloch*, Kamac Publications, Dublin, 1982.

Macleod, Kenneth *The Road to the Isles*, Robert Grant, 1927.

Mackey, James P. *Introduction to Celtic Christianity*, T. and T. Clark, Edinburgh, 1989.

Maher, Michael, ed. *Irish Spirituality*, Veritas Publications, Dublin, 1981.

Matthews, Caitlin *The Elements of the Celtic Tradition*, Element Books, 1989.

Mould, D.D.C.P. *Ireland and the Saints*, Batsford, 1953.

—*The Celtic Saints, Our Heritage*, Burns, Oates and Washbourne, 1956.

—*The Irish Saints* Burns & Oates, 1964.

—*The Monasteries of Ireland* Batsford, 1976.

O'Meara, John J. *The Voyage of St Brendan*, Dolmen Press, 1985.

Porter, H.M. *The Celtic Church in Somerset*, Morgan Books, Bath, 1971.

Rees, Alwyn and Brinley *Celtic Heritage: Ancient Tradition in Ireland and Wales*, Thames and Hudson, 1961.

Stewart, Columba OSB *The World of the Desert Fathers*, SLG Press, Oxford, 1986.

Thomas, Patrick *The Opened Door: A Celtic Spirituality*, Silyn Publications, 1990.

Toulson, Shirley *Celtic Journeys*, Random Century, 1985.

—*The Celtic Alternative*, Random Century, 1987.

—*The Winter Solstice*, Jill Norman and Hobhouse, 1981.

Van den Weyer, Robert *Celtic Fire*, Darton, Longman & Todd, 1990.

Ward, Benedicta *The Wisdom of the Desert Fathers*, SLG Press, Oxford, 1981.

 # Index of Saints

 # General Index